The Observer's Pocket Series

SEA FISHES

The Observer Books

A POCKET REFERENCE SERIES COVERING A
WIDE RANGE OF SUBJECTS

Natural History

BIRDS
BIRDS' EGGS
BUTTERFLIES
LARGER MOTHS
COMMON INSECTS
WILD ANIMALS
ZOO ANIMALS
WILD FLOWERS
GARDEN FLOWERS
FLOWERING TREES
          AND SHRUBS
HOUSE PLANTS
CACTI
TREES
GRASSES
COMMON FUNGI
LICHENS
POND LIFE
FRESHWATER FISHES
SEA FISHES
SEA AND SEASHORE
GEOLOGY
ASTRONOMY
WEATHER
CATS
DOGS
HORSES AND PONIES

Transport

AIRCRAFT
AUTOMOBILES
COMMERCIAL VEHICLES
SHIPS
MANNED SPACEFLIGHT
UNMANNED SPACEFLIGHT
MOTOR SPORT
BRITISH STEAM LOCOMOTIVES

The Arts etc.

ARCHITECTURE
CATHEDRALS
CHURCHES
HERALDRY
FLAGS
PAINTING
MODERN ART
SCULPTURE
FURNITURE
POTTERY AND PORCELAIN
MUSIC
POSTAGE STAMPS
EUROPEAN COSTUME
BRITISH AWARDS AND MEDALS

Sport

ASSOCIATION FOOTBALL
CRICKET

Cities

LONDON

The Observer's Book of

SEA FISHES

T. B. BAGENAL, M.A.

DESCRIBING 215 SPECIES
WITH 139 ILLUSTRATIONS
OF WHICH 32 ARE IN FULL COLOUR

FREDERICK WARNE & CO LTD
FREDERICK WARNE & CO INC
LONDON : NEW YORK

ISBN 0 7232 1509 x

Printed in Great Britain by
William Clowes & Sons, Limited
London, Beccles and Colchester

Preface

Since the previous edition of this book was written, many years ago, a great deal has been added to our knowledge of British sea fishes. Not only has a large amount of research been done on commercially important species, but also there has been a great upsurge in interest in all forms of natural history and this has led to more awareness of the smaller species, particularly those living on the shore. Another factor is that the occurrence of rare species may indicate movements of large water masses, often over considerable distances, from regions where the fish are common. These freak currents may affect our fisheries, and for this reason rare fish have been studied in greater detail than hitherto. Because of the increased knowledge of all our fish, it was decided that the book should be completely rewritten.

I wish to thank the National Anglers' Council and the British Record (rod-caught) Fish Committee for permission to quote the most recent record weights.

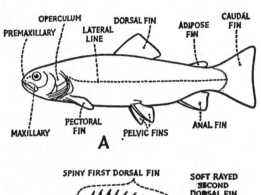

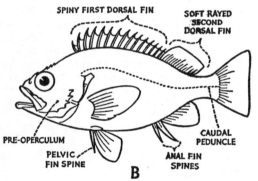

Introduction

This book is intended to help in the identification of sea fishes that are found around Britain. It is written mainly for the general naturalist, but I hope that it will also aid the angler in naming his catch correctly and assist school parties in carrying out natural history field-work.

The British Isles are in a very favourable position from the ichthyological point of view. Not only do we have the native species that breed around our coasts, but many stragglers also come to our shores. A number of species that are normally found in the Mediterranean and Spanish Atlantic coast occasionally come as far north as Britain. Similarly, Arctic species of Iceland and Norway may extend south to the British Isles. Lastly, there are oceanic species which get carried to us from the deep Atlantic by the Gulf Stream and North Atlantic Drift. From this it is evident that a great many species occur naturally round the British Isles. In addition, there are many alien species brought to the fish markets by our large and wide-ranging fishing fleets.

In this book I have mentioned as many species as possible, even if they are rare and only a word or two can be spared on them. Although young people and beginners need to learn the names and habits of our common species, everyone turns to a reference book when confronted with an unusual fish, and this is when help is required. I have tried to include all the kinds of fish that might be caught by anglers, found by the naturalist, or seen at the fishmonger's.

It must be emphasized that the identification of all rare fish should be checked by an expert, and the staff of the British Museum (Natural History), South Kensington, London, are always willing to help with difficult species, *provided* the specimens are properly preserved. It is absolutely essential that the fish is preserved in methylated spirit or dilute formalin (both can be obtained from a chemist) for three days and then packed damp, in a polythene bag. Only then may it be posted. Neither the experts nor the Post Office like a mass of rotten and stinking fish. All that is asked for in return for the help in identifying and commenting on your fish is that these few and simple instructions are obeyed.

In this book a description of the form and colours of each fish is given, and the features that distinguish it from similar species are stressed. The usual lengths and weights are stated in both metric and imperial units. Notes are given on the habitat, breeding habits, food, distribution and other general natural history features, together with details of the economic importance of the fish. Technical terms and jargon have been avoided as far as possible, but where necessary the reader should refer to the diagrams on page vi.

Classified Index to
Orders, Families, Genera and Species

Class *MARSIPOBRANCHII*

Order HYPEROARTIA

Order HYPEROTRETA

Class *SELACHII*

Order PLEUROTREMATA

Family SCYLIORHINIDAE

    Greater-spotted dog-   *Scyliorhinus stellaris* (L.),
    fish   p. 32
    Lesser-spotted dogfish   *Scyliorhinus caniculus* (L.),
        p. 33
    Black-mouthed dogfish   *Galeus melastomus* Rafin-
        esque-Schmaltz, p. 34

Family SPHYRNIDAE

    Hammerhead shark   *Sphyrna zygaena* (L.),
        p. 34

Family ISURIDAE

    Porbeagle   *Lamna nasus* (Bonnaterre)
        p. 35
    Mako   *Isurus oxyrinchus* Rafin-
        esque-Schmaltz, p. 35

Family CETORHINIDAE
    Basking shark   *Cetorhinus maximus*
        (Gunnerus), p. 36

Family ALOPIIDAE

    Thresher shark   *Alopias vulpinus* (Bonna-
        terre), p. 37

Family CARCHARINIDAE

    Blue shark   *Prionace glauca* (L.), p. 38
    Tope   *Galeorhinus galeus* (L.),
        p. 39

Family TRIAKIDAE

Smooth hound   *Mustelus mustelus* (L.),
p. 39
Mustelus asterias Cloquet,
p. 40

Family SQUALIDAE

Spur-dog   *Squalus acanthias* (L.),
p. 40

Bramble shark   *Echinorhinus brucus*
(Bonnaterre), p. 42

Greenland shark   *Somniosus microcephalus*
(Bloch and Schneider),
p. 41

Darkie charlie   *Dalatias licha* (Bonnaterre), p. 42

Family OXYNOTIDAE

Oxynotus paradoxus Frade,
p. 42

Family SQUATINIDAE

Monkfish   *Squatina squatina* (L.),
p. 42

5

Order HYPOTREMATA

Family TORPEDINIDAE

Electric ray
    Torpedo nobiliana Bonaparte, p. 43
    Torpedo marmorata Risso, p. 44

Family RAJIDAE

Common skate	*Raja batis* L., p. 47
Shagreen skate	*Raja fullonica* L., p. 48
Long-nosed skate	*Raja oxyrinchus* L., p. 48
White skate	*Raja alba* Lacépède, p. 48
Thornback ray	*Raja clavata* L., p. 49
Undulate ray	*Raja undulata* Lacépède, p. 49
Cuckoo ray	*Raja naevus* Müller and Henle, p. 50
Starry ray	*Raja radiata* Donovan, p. 50
Sandy ray	*Raja circularis* Couch, p. 50
Spotted ray	*Raja montagui* Fowler, p. 51
Painted ray	*Raja microocellata* Montagu, p. 51
Blonde	*Raja brachyura* Lafont, p. 51

6

Family DASYATIDAE

Sting ray   *Dasyatis pastinaca* (L.), p. 52

Family MYLIOBATIDAE

Eagle ray   *Myliobatis aquila* (L.), p. 53-

Order CHIMAEREA

Family CHIMAERIDAE

Rabbit-fish   *Chimaera monstrosa* L., p. 54

Class *PISCES*

Order CHONDROSTEI

Family ACIPENSERIDAE

Sturgeon   *Acipenser sturio* L., p. 55

Order ISOSPONDYLI

Family CLUPEIDAE

Allis shad	*Alosa alosa* (L.), p. 56
Twaite shad	*Alosa fallax* (Lacépède), p. 56
Pilchard	*Sardina pilchardus* (Walbaum), p. 57
Sprat	*Sprattus sprattus* (L.), p. 58
Herring	*Clupea harengus* L., p. 59
Anchovy	*Engraulis encrasicolus* (L.), p. 63

Family SALMONIDAE

Salmon	*Salmo salar* L., p. 64
Sea trout	*Salmo trutta* L., p. 65

Family OSMERIDAE

Smelt	*Osmerus eperlanus* (L.), p. 66

Family ARGENTINIDAE

Argentine	*Argentina sphyraena* L., p. 67

Order APODES

Family ANGUILLIDAE

Common eel	*Anguilla anguilla* (L.), p. 67

Family CONGRIDAE

  Conger eel   *Conger conger* (L.), p. 69

Family MURAENIDAE

  Moray eel   *Muraena helena* L., p. 70

Order SYNENTOGNATHI

Family BELONIDAE

  Garfish   *Belone bellone* (L.), p. 70

Family SCOMBERESOCIDAE

  Saury pike   *Scomberesox saurus* (Walbaum), p. 71

Order SOLENICHTHYES

Family SYNGNATHIDAE

  Great pipefish   *Syngnathus acus* L., p. 73
  Broad-nosed pipefish   *Syngnathus typhle* L., p. 74
  Lesser pipefish   *Syngnathus rostellatus* Nilsson, p. 74

Snake pipefish	*Entelurus aequoreus* (L.), p. 74
Worm pipefish	*Nerophis lumbriciformis* (Jenyns), p. 74
Straight-nosed pipe-fish	*Nerophis ophidion* (L.), p. 74
Sea-horse	*Hippocampus ramulosus* Leach, p. 75

Order ANACANTHINI

Family GADIDAE

Cod	*Gadus morhua* L., p. 76
Haddock	*Melanogrammus aeglefinus* (L.), p. 78
Whiting	*Merlangius merlangus* (L.), p. 79
Saithe	*Pollachius virens* (L.), p. 81
Pollack	*Pollachius pollachius* (L.), p. 81
Bib	*Trisopterus luscus* (L.), p. 82
Poor cod	*Trisopterus minutus* (L.), p. 83
Norway pout	*Trisopterus esmarkii* (Nilsson), p. 84

Hake

	Merluccius merluccius (L.), p. 85
Ling	*Molva molva* (L.), p. 86
Blue ling	*Molva dypterygia* (Pennant), p. 88
Greater fork-beard	*Phycis blennoides* (Brünnich), p. 88

Order ALLOTRIOGNATHI

Family LAMPRIDIDAE

Family TRACHIPTERIDAE

Order ZEOMORPHI

Family ZEIDAE

Family CAPROIDAE

Boar-fish   *Capros aper* (L.), p. 95

Order PERCOMORPHI

Family SERRANIDAE

Bass   *Dicentrarchus labrax* (L.),
                              p. 96
Wreck fish   *Polyprion americanus*
                              (Bloch and Schneider),
                              p. 98
Comber   *Serranus cabrilla* (L.), p.
                              98
Dusky perch   *Epinephelus guaza* (L.),
                              p. 98

Family CARANGIDAE

Amberjack   *Seriola dumerili* (Risso),
                              p. 99
Pilot fish   *Naucrates ductor* (L.), p.
                              99
Derbio   *Trachinotus ovatus* (L.),
                              p. 99
Horse mackerel   *Trachurus trachurus* (L.),
                              p. 99

| Family BRAMIDAE | |

Long-finned bream   *Taractes   longipinnis* (Lowe), p. 101
                              Taractes asper Lowe, p. 101
                              Pterycombus brama Fries, p. 101

Ray's bream   *Brama brama* (Bonnaterre), p. 101

| Family SCIAENIDAE | |

Meagre   *Argyrosomus regium* (Asso), p. 102

| Family MULLIDAE | |

Red mullet   *Mullus surmuletus* L., p. 103
                          Mullus barbatus L., p. 103

| Family SPARIDAE | |

Red sea bream   *Pagellus bogaraveo* (Brünnich), p. 104

Pandora   *Pagellus erythrinus* (L.), p. 106

Spanish bream	*Pagellus acarne* (Risso), p. 107
Black sea bream	*Spondyliosoma cantharus* (L.), p. 105
Bogue	*Boops boops* (L.), p. 106
Gilt-head	*Sparus aurata* L., p. 106
Dentex	*Dentex dentex* (L.), p. 107
Pagre	*Pagrus pagrus* (L.), p. 107

Family CEPOLIDAE

| Red band-fish | *Cepola rubescens* L., p. 107 |

Family LABRIDAE

Ballan wrasse	*Labrus bergylta* Ascanius, p. 108
Cuckoo wrasse	*Labrus mixtus* L., p. 109
Rainbow wrasse	*Coris julis* (L.), p. 109
Scale-rayed wrasse	*Acantholabrus palloni* (Risso), p. 110
Rock cook	*Centrolabrus exoletus* (L.), p. 110
Goldsinny	*Ctenolabrus rupestris* (L.), p. 110
Corkwing	*Crenilabrus melops* (L.), p. 111

Family AMMODYTIDAE

Lesser sandeel	*Ammodytes tobianus* L., p. 112
Raitt's sandeel	*Ammodytes marinus* Raitt, p. 113
Greater sandeel	*Hyperoplus lanceolatus* (Lesauvage), p. 112

| Corbin's sandeel | *Hyperoplus immaculatus* (Corbin), p. 113 |
| Smooth sandeel | *Gymnammodytes semi-squamatus* (Jourdain), p. 113 |

Family TRACHINIDAE

| Lesser weever | *Trachinus vipera* Cuvier, p. 114 |
| Greater weever | *Trachinus draco* L., p. 115 |

Family SCOMBRIDAE

Mackerel	*Scomber scombrus* L., p. 116
Spanish mackerel	*Scomber colias* Gmelin, p. 119
Tunny	*Thunnus thynnus* (L.), p. 118
Long-finned tunny	*Thunnus alalunga* (Bonnaterre), p. 119
Bonito	*Sarda sarda* (Bloch), p. 119
Oceanic bonito	*Katsuwonus pelamis* (L.), p. 119
Frigate mackerel	*Auxis thazard* (Lacépède), p. 119

Family XIPHIIDAE

| Swordfish | *Xiphias gladius* L., p. 120 |

Family GOBIIDAE

Crystal goby	*Crystallogobius linearis* (Düben), p. 122
Transparent goby	*Aphia minuta* (Risso), p. 122
Two-spot goby	*Chaparrudo flavescens* (Fabricius), p. 122
Common goby	*Pomatoschistus microps* (Krøyer), p. 123
Sand goby	*Pomatoschistus minutus* (Pallas), p. 123
Painted goby	*Pomatoschistus pictus* (Malm), p. 124
Black goby	*Gobius niger* L., p. 124
Rock goby	*Gobius paganellus* L., p. 125
Giant goby	*Gobius cobitis* Pallas, p. 125
	Gobius cruentatus Gmelin, p. 126
Leopard-spotted goby	*Thorogobius ephippiatus* (Lowe), p. 126
Fries' goby	*Lesueurigobius friesii* (Collett), p. 125
Jeffrey's goby	*Buenia jeffreysii* (Günther), p. 126
Diminutive goby	*Lebetus orca* (Collett), p. 126

Family CALLIONYMIDAE

Common dragonet	*Callionymus lyra* L., p. 127

| Spotted dragonet | *Callionymus maculatus* Rafinesque-Schmaltz, p. 128 |
| | *Callionymus reticulatus* Valenciennes, p. 128 |

Family BLENNIIDAE

Shanny	*Blennius pholis* L., p. 129
Tompot blenny	*Blennius gattorugine* L., p. 130
Butterfly blenny	*Blennius ocellaris* L., p. 130
Montagu's blenny	*Coryphoblennius galerita* (L.), p. 130

Family PHOLIDIDAE

| Butterfish | *Pholis gunnellus* (L.), p. 131 |

Family STICHAEIDAE

| Yarrell's blenny | *Chirolophis ascanii* (Walbaum), p. 132 |

Family LUMPENIDAE

| Snake blenny | *Lumpenus lumpretaeformis* (Walbaum), p. 132 |

17

Family ZOARCIDAE

    Viviparous blenny   *Zoarces viviparus* (L.), p. 133

Family ANARHICHADIDAE

    Catfish   *Anarhichas lupus* L., p. 134
    Spotted catfish   *Anarhichas minor* Olafsen, p. 135

Family CENTROLOPHIDAE

    Black-fish   *Centrolophus niger* (Gmelin), p. 135

Family MUGILIDAE

    Thick-lipped mullet   *Crenimugil labrosus* (Risso), p. 136
    Thin-lipped mullet   *Liza ramada* (Risso), p. 137
    Golden mullet   *Liza auratus* (Risso), p. 136

Family ATHERINIDAE

    Sand smelt   *Atherina presbyter* Valenciennes, p. 139
    Boyer's sand smelt   *Atherina mochon* Valenciennes, p. 139

Order SCLEROPAREI

Family SCORPAENIDAE

Red-fish   *Sebastes marinus* (L.), p. 140

                 Sebastes viviparus Krøyer, p. 140

Blue-mouth   *Helicolenus dactylopterus* (Delaroche), p. 141

Family TRIGLIDAE

Grey gurnard   *Eutrigla gurnardus* (L.), p. 142

Tub gurnard   *Trigla lucerna* L., p. 143

Piper   *Trigla lyra* L., p. 144

Red gurnard   *Aspitrigla cuculus* (L.), p. 143

Long-finned gurnard   *Aspitrigla obscura* (L.), p. 144

Streaked gurnard   *Trigloporus lastoviza* (Bonnaterre), p. 144

Family COTTIDAE

Short-spined sea-scorpion   *Myoxocephalus scorpius* (L.), p. 144

Long-spined sea-scorpion   *Taurulus bubalis* (Euphrasen), p. 145

Norway bullhead   *Taurulus lilljeborgi* (Collett), p. 146

                 Triglops murrayi Günther, p. 146

Family AGONIDAE

Pogge   *Agonus cataphractus* (L.), p. 147

Family CYCLOPTERIDAE

Lumpsucker   *Cyclopterus lumpus* L., p. 147

Family LIPARIDAE

Sea snail   *Liparis liparis* (L.), p. 149
Montagu's sea snail   *Liparis montagui* (Donovan), p. 149

Family GASTEROSTEIDAE

Ten-spined stickle-   *Pungitius pungitius* (L.),
    back   p. 150
Three-spined stickle-   *Gasterosteus aculeatus* L.,
    back   p. 150
Fifteen-spined stickle-   *Spinachia spinachia* (L.),
    back   p. 151

Order HETEROSOMATA

Family BOTHIDAE

Turbot   *Scophthalmus maximus* (L.), p. 153
Brill   *Scophthalmus rhombus* (L.), p. 154

Topknot	*Zeugopterus punctatus* (Bloch), p. 155
Bloch's topknot	*Phrynorhombus regius* (Bonnaterre), p. 155
Norwegian topknot	*Phrynorhombus norvegicus* (Günther), p. 156
Megrim	*Lepidorhombus whiffi-agonis* (Walbaum), p.156 *Lepidorhombus boscii* (Risso), p. 157
Scaldfish	*Arnoglossus laterna* (Walbaum), p. 157 *Arnoglossus thori* Kyle, p. 157 *Arnoglossus imperialis* (Rafinesque-Schmaltz), p. 157

Family PLEURONECTIDAE

Plaice	*Pleuronectes platessa* L., p. 158
Dab	*Limanda limanda* (L.), p. 160
Flounder	*Platichthys flesus* (L.), p. 161
Lemon sole	*Microstomus kitt* (Walbaum), p. 162
Witch	*Glyptocephalus cynoglossus* (L.), p. 163
Long rough dab	*Hippoglossoides platessoides* (Fabricius), p. 164
Halibut	*Hippoglossus hippoglossus* (L.), p. 165

| Greenland halibut | *Reinhardtius hippoglossoides* (Walbaum), p. 165 |

Family SOLEIDAE

Sole	*Solea solea* (L.), p. 166
Sand sole	*Pegusa lascaris* (Risso), p. 168
Solenette	*Buglossidium luteum* (Risso), p. 168
Thick-back sole	*Microchirus variegatus* (Donovan), p. 169

Order PLECTOGNATHI

Family BALISTIDAE

| Triggerfish | *Balistes carolinensis* (Gmelin), p. 169 |

Family TETRAODONTIDAE

| Puffer-fish | *Lagocephalus lagocephalus* (L.), p. 170 |

Family MOLIDAE

Sunfish   *Mola mola* (L.), p. 170
Truncated sunfish   *Ranzania laevis* (Pennant)
                p. 171

Order XENOPTERYGII

Family GOBIESOCIDAE

Small-headed clingfish   *Apletodon microcephalus*
                        (Brook), p. 172
Two-spotted clingfish   *Diplecogaster bimaculata*
                        (Bonnaterre), p. 172
Shore clingfish   *Lepadogaster lepadogaster*
                        (Bonnaterre), p. 172
Connemara clingfish   *Lepadogaster candollei*
                        Risso, p. 173

Order PEDICULATI

Family LOPHIIDAE

Angler fish   *Lophius piscatorius* L., p
                      173

Class *MARSIPOBRANCHII*

The Lampreys   PETROMYZONIDAE

The lampreys belong to a primitive group of
fish-like creatures called the Agnatha, which
means 'without jaws'. The Agnatha formed the
dominant fish group during the Devonian period,
350–400 million years ago. Most of the species
became extinct, but from some of them the cartilaginous and bony fishes with jaws have evolved.
However, the lampreys and hagfishes are sur-
vivors of the Agnatha and are of great interest to
zoologists because they show some characteristics
which it is thought were possessed by all the
Agnatha. Besides having no jaws, the lampreys
have no bones, no scales and no paired fins, and
they have only a simple arrangement of the kid-
neys and nerves. In addition to these primitive
characteristics, the lampreys have extremely
specialized methods of feeding and breeding, and
their suckers are highly evolved features.

The lampreys are similar to eels, but their lack
of paired fins, the arrangement of their gills, the
two dorsal fins and the sucker should prevent
confusion (see Plate 1).

The **sea lamprey**, *Petromyzon marinus*
(Plate 1), is the largest and the most marine of
the three British species. It grows to 90 cm
(36 in.) in length and about 7·5 cm (3 in.) in

thickness. The sucker is large and powerful with rows of hooked teeth and a rasping tongue. After fastening on to its prey, the fish rasps through the skin and sucks the victim's blood. Mouth secretions begin to digest the prey even before it is eaten. Fish often attacked are cod, haddock, salmon and basking sharks, as well as a wide variety of others.

The eye is large and followed by a series of seven gill openings. The gills are in pockets supported on a cage of elastic gristle. The water is forced out of the pockets by the contraction of muscles. When these relax the pockets expand, owing to the elasticity of the gristle, and water is drawn in. This muscular pumping action is very rapid and is characteristic of living lampreys.

The lack of paired fins has already been mentioned. The unpaired fins consist of two well-separated dorsal fins and a caudal fin. In the breeding season the male develops a ridge along the back and the female grows a small fin behind the vent.

The colour of the sea lamprey is quite distinct from that of the other species. The back is dark, with irregular-shaped brown blotches on a reddish or olive-brown background. The underparts are a greyish white.

Sea lampreys spend one or two years at sea and when mature, at about 70 cm (28 in.), migrate into swift-flowing rivers where the bottom is gravelly. Each pair constructs a nest by lifting stones with their suckers from an area of about 60 × 90 cm (2 × 3 ft). The eggs are laid in this nest. The adults are completely emaciated after spawning and they all die.

The larvae which hatch from the eggs drift downstream to a place where the current is slack and the bottom is a fine mud. Here they live buried in the mud, feeding on minute particles of detritus (small bits of animals and plants). They are blind and toothless, and are called ammocoete larvae. They are so unlike the adults in general appearance that they were at one time thought to be a completely different kind of animal and were called *Ammocoetes branchialis*.

After about five years the ammocoetes metamorphose into the adult form at 15–20 cm (6–8 in.) and migrate to the sea to start their parasitic life.

The sea lamprey is found all round the British Isles but is more plentiful in the south. Breeding takes place in unpolluted rivers which are fast flowing over coarse stony gravel and which also have slack muddy areas downstream. The lampreys also require reasonable access, without obstacles such as weirs.

The **river lamprey**, *Lampetra fluviatilis* (Plate 1), is smaller than the sea lamprey. It grows to 50 cm (20 in.) in length and 3 cm (1¼ in.) in thickness. It also has a powerful sucker with sharp teeth and a rasping tongue. Behind the eye are seven gill chambers. The colour is quite distinct from that of the sea lamprey. The upper parts are a dark slaty brown or olive grey. The underparts are a dirty creamy white. There are no paired fins and the two dorsal fins are well separated, except at the breeding season when they join.

The river lamprey probably spends a year and a half at sea as a parasite on other fish, but it does not go so far out to sea as the larger species. As lampreys mature they migrate to the spawning rivers; they stop feeding and the gut atrophies. The migration usually takes place in autumn and early winter, and spawning occurs in about April. A nest similar to that of the sea lamprey is built, but the stones are smaller. The eggs hatch to give ammocoete larvae which live in rich mud downstream of the spawning area. After four to five years they metamorphose into small lampreys of about 12 cm ($4\frac{3}{4}$ in.) and they migrate to the sea. They are found round the shores of Britain south of the Caledonian Canal, but are not common.

The amount of pollution probably restricts the number of rivers that are suitable for spawning, for both species, and the resulting scarcity of these fish means that they are not a serious threat to fisheries. However, when the Welland Canal was built in North America to by-pass the Niagara Falls, sea lampreys invaded the Great Lakes and developed a completely freshwater life history. They became abundant and caused a catastrophic decline in the lake fisheries.

The Hagfishes   MYXINIDAE

The **hagfish**, *Myxine glutinosa*, is another very primitive fish without jaws, scales or paired fins, but which has a specialized scavenging mode of life. There is no sucker round the mouth, but it has three pairs of barbels and a single nostril on the tip of the snout. It has a continuous fin from the vent to the top of the tail. The hagfish has biting teeth which penetrate the skin of its dead prey, which is devoured, leaving only skin and bones. The hagfish also eats a variety of invertebrates, and fish. It is rare round most of Britain, and grows to 50 cm (20 in.), but is usually about 30 cm (12 in.).

Class *SELACHII*

The Selachians are fishes with cartilaginous skeletons as distinct from the Teleosts, which are true fishes with bony skeletons. Cartilage is a gristly substance, but often it may become hardened and calcified with age so that it can be difficult to distinguish, at first sight, from true bone. In most species there are several gill slits behind the head, but in the skates they are below the head. The skin is often very rough with numerous small tooth-like structures called 'dermal denticles' embedded in it. The shape of the denticles is often characteristic of the species, but is a feature most suited to the professional zoologist rather than the field naturalist. The males have conspicuous copulatory organs, called the claspers, on the inner sides of the pelvic fins. That part of the brain known as the olefactory lobes, associated with the sense of smell, is well developed in all the species. These fish hunt in packs.

Some of the Selachians are oviparous, that is, they lay eggs. An example is the lesser-spotted dogfish. Others are viviparous, that is, they give birth to live, fully formed young which have developed with nutriment from the mother, to whom they are intimately attached by a placenta (e.g. the blue shark). Many of the selachians are ovoviviparous; the embryos are not connected directly to the mother, but they continue to develop in the egg within her, feeding partly on their food reserves (the yolk) and partly on nourishment secreted by the mother. They are born as fully-formed young.

The class is divided into two sub-classes, the Euselachii, the sharks, dogfish and skates; and the Holocephali, the rabbit-fishes.

Two rare sharks can also be mentioned before we deal with the more usual selachians. The **six-gilled shark**, *Hexanchus griseus*, is caught by trawlers or by rod and line about five times a year, mainly off County Kerry. It can be recognized by its six gill slits, none of which is joined under the throat. It has a single dorsal fin. The even rarer **frilled shark**, *Chlamydoselachus anguineus*, is a very long and thin shark with six gill slits with frilly margins, the first of which joins under the throat.

The Spotted Dogfishes   SCYLIORHINIDAE

The two common species in this family that are found in British waters are the greater-spotted dogfish and the lesser-spotted dogfish. There are many other English names for them and this leads to considerable confusion. In southern England the larger species is often called the nurse hound, and the smaller species is just called the dogfish. However in Scotland, where the larger species is very rare, the smaller species is the nurse, and the name dogfish is used for *Squalus acanthias*, which is quite a different fish in a different family. Elsewhere the larger species is called the nurse hound, bull huss, catfish, bounce or huss. It is perhaps least confusing to use a name based on their different sizes, though greater-spotted dogfish is rather a mouthful to come often in a conversation.

The **greater-spotted dogfish**, *Scyliorhinus stellaris* (Plate 5), has a few large rounded dark brown spots on a grey background, and the belly is a creamy white. The skin is very rough. The most reliable characteristic for distinguishing the spotted dogfishes is the shape of the nasal flap, and this is described for them both under the next species.

The greater-spotted dogfish grows to 150 cm (60 in.) and 9·5 kg (21 lb). The British rod-caught record is 9·61 kg (21 lb 3 oz) for one caught off Looe, in 1955.

The greater-spotted dogfish lays large eggs, each of which is in a horny rectangular capsule known as a mermaid's purse. The eggs are laid near low tide. The empty cases are very often cast up on the shore. There is a pair of twining filaments at each end of the capsule. The female swims around a tangle of seaweeds or stones while laying the eggs, until the filaments get entangled and she can swim away leaving the eggs attached. The eggs of *S. stellaris* are about 12 cm (4¾ in.) long. The young are 16 cm (6¼ in.) long when they hatch.

The greater-spotted dogfish feeds on squid and bottom-living fish such as dragonets, flatfish and gurnards, as well as crabs and other crustaceans.

The **lesser-spotted dogfish,** *Scyliorhinus caniculus* (Plate 5), has many small dark brown spots on a lighter brown background and the belly is pale. The colours of both species, however, can be variable and the best feature for identifying them is the shape of the nasal flaps. These lie behind the nostrils on the underside of the head. In the greater-spotted dogfish the flaps are not joined across the middle and do not extend as far back as the mouth. In the lesser-spotted species the flaps join in the middle and extend over the front of the lower jaw.

The lesser-spotted dogfish reaches 76 cm (30 in.) and 4·5 kg (10 lb), which is half the size of the larger species. The British rod-caught record is 2·041 kg (4½ lb) for one caught off Ayr pier in 1969.

The breeding of the lesser-spotted dogfish is very similar to that described for the larger species. The eggs are 5–6·5 cm (2–2½ in.) long and are more rounded as well as being smaller, and the young at hatching are only 10 cm (4 in.). As in the other species, mating takes place in deep water in late summer and egg-laying is mainly throughout the winter and spring.

The lesser-spotted dogfish is extremely common all round Britain. It frequents hard sandy and rocky ground from 5 to 100 m (3 to 55 fathoms). Its food consists of many invertebrates such as the whelk, scallop, clam and other bivalves, and crustacea such as shrimps, prawns, crabs and hermit crabs. The fish that are eaten are small, for example gobies, young dabs and plaice.

The greater- and lesser-spotted dogfishes, together with the spur-dog (page 40), make up the 'dogfishes' of commercial landings. These are of considerable economic importance. In 1972, 14,400 tons, with a gross value of £928,000, were landed at British ports. They will have been sold mainly as 'rock eel' or 'rock salmon', and are regularly used in fish and chip shops. The Selachians excrete nitrogen in the form of urea and this gives them their characteristic taste. Although dogfish have many devotees, most people prefer the finer flavour of cod, haddock or plaice.

A less common third species in this family is the **black-mouthed dogfish**, *Galeus melastomus*. The back has a pattern of connected dark brown blotches with lighter borders, and the inside of the mouth is black. This fish is found in deep water along the edge of the continental shelf and grows to about 75 cm (30 in.).

The Hammerhead Shark SPHYRNIDAE

The **hammerhead shark**, *Sphyrna zygaena*, *is* an extraordinarily shaped fish. The head is flattened and has lobes on each side. The eyes and nostrils are on the ends of these lobes, which may enable the shark to see and smell over a wider area. The hammerhead grows to 4 m (13 ft), but is a very rare British fish.

The Mackerel Sharks ISURIDAE

The **porbeagle**, *Lamna nasus* (Plate 4), is a large shark, growing to 3 m (10 ft) in length and 180 kg (400 lb) in weight. The British rod-caught record is for a shark of 195·036 kg (430 lb) caught south of Jersey in 1969. The porbeagle can be recognized by its rounded snout and keel-like ridges along each side of the tail. The first dorsal fin is above the base of the pectorals.

Porbeagles are recorded from all round the British Isles, but are most frequently found off the Cornish coast in summertime, where they migrate from more southerly oceanic waters.

The porbeagle has no commercial value in Britain and when caught it is usually a considerable nuisance. Often it breaks through the fisherman's net leaving a huge rent, or it eats the catches from long lines. However, in recent years, a sport fishery for porbeagles has become very popular at Looe in Cornwall.

Its food consists of shoaling pelagic fish such as herring, mackerel, pilchard and also cod, pollack, flatfish and whiting, as well as dogfish.

The porbeagle is ovoviviparous; the young are said to be 50 cm (20 in.) when born.

A shark very similar to the porbeagle is the **mako**, *Isurus oxyrinchus*. It grows to a similar size and can be distinguished by its dorsal fin, which is set well behind the base of the pectoral fin, and its more pointed snout. It is a more southern species than the porbeagle, and is considerably rarer. It was only in 1955 that this species was recognized as British; before then it had been confused with the porbeagle. The British rod-caught record is for one of 226·786 kg (500 lb) caught off the Eddystone Lighthouse in 1971.

The Basking Shark   CETORHINIDAE

The **basking shark**, *Cetorhinus maximus* (Plate 2), is one of the largest British fishes. It grows to 12 m (40 ft) and may have a weight of well over 3000 kg (3 tons). Its size alone is sufficient for identification at sea, but it has two other characteristics associated with its feeding.

Like the baleen whales, the food of these vast creatures consists of minute planktonic organisms. These are very small copepods, euphausids, crustacean larvae, the eggs and larvae of fish, and larvae of many other groups which drift in the middle and upper water layers. The basking shark has a huge mouth and large gill slits which extend from near the top of the head to under the throat. The fish swims along with its mouth open, and the plankton is sieved out of the water on stiff bristle-like gill rakers as it passes through the gill slits.

The huge gill slits and bristle-like gill rakers are quite characteristic of the basking shark. Plankton is a very rich source of food, and animals that feed largely on plankton (that is herrings and whales) tend to be rich in oils (or blubber). This is also the case with the basking shark, whose liver is very oily and is said to make up to one-third of the total body weight. At various times basking sharks have been hunted on the west coasts for the sake of their liver oil.

Basking sharks are found mainly on the western side of the British Isles, and appear inshore during the summer off the coasts of western Ireland and Scotland, where they swim lazily about with their mouth open collecting plankton. In winter, they shed their gill rakers and remain on the seabed until new ones have grown and plankton has become plentiful again.

Basking sharks are viviparous and although very little is known definitely about their breeding biology, it has been suggested that the young are 150 cm (60 in.) at birth and that they grow to about 3 m (10 ft) in the first year.

The Thresher Shark   ALOPIIDAE

The **thresher shark**, *Alopias vulpinus* (Plate 2), is immediately recognized by its enormously long curved tail whose scythe-shaped upper lobe may extend up to half the total body length. It grows to 6 m (20 ft). The British rod-caught record is at 127 kg (280 lb) for one caught off Dungeness in 1933.

The thresher is fairly common round western Britain, particularly in summer when there is a migration from warmer southern waters. Its food consists of pelagic herring, mackerel and similar fish which it herds into a dense shoal by means of its tail, before eating them.

Very little is known about the breeding biology of the thresher except that it is ovoviviparous and the young are relatively small.

The Blue Shark and Tope   CARCHARINIDAE

The **blue shark**, *Prionace glauca* (Plate 3), is a popular sport fish in south-west England, based mainly on Looe during the summer. The British rod-caught record blue shark of 98·878 kg (218 lb) was caught off Looe in 1959.

It is normally found in semi-tropical waters, but migrates in summer to European coasts. In some years this migration extends further north than in others, but the sharks rarely reach the north of Scotland in any numbers.

This shark has a dark indigo-blue back, a long curved pectoral fin and a longish pointed snout. The main food consists of herring, mackerel and pilchards, and in the pursuit of these the sharks often get entangled in fishing nets and completely wreck them.

The blue shark is viviparous and there is a placenta from the developing embryo to the uterus of the mother.

The **tope**, *Galeorhinus galeus* (Plate 4), is smaller than the typical shark and larger than a dogfish. It grows to 2 m (6½ ft). The British rod-caught record tope weighed 33·876 kg (74 lb 11 oz) and was caught at Caldy Island in 1964. The colour is a slate grey on the back and lighter on the belly.

This fish is fairly common round the British Isles and has a northerly distribution, right round the Scottish north coast to Norway and through the North Sea. The tope is also found in shallower, less oceanic water than the larger sharks and it is present, though more offshore, throughout the winter. The tope is mainly a bottom-living fish, and this is where it catches its food such as dabs, plaice, flounders and dragonets; herring, whiting and other mid-water gadids are also eaten.

Tope are viviparous, and as many as thirty-two young may obtain their nourishment from the mother at one time.

The Smooth Hounds TRIAKIDAE

The **smooth hound** consists of two species, *Mustelus mustelus* (Plate 3) and *M. asterias*. The former has white spots and the latter has none. Otherwise the dull grey colouring on the back, shading to creamy white below, is the same in both species. They both grow to 120 cm (4 ft). The British rod-caught record for *M. mustelus* stands at 12·7 kg (28 lb) for one caught at Heacham in 1969.

The most significant difference between the species is that *M. mustelus* is viviparous, with a direct connection between the young in the uterus and its mother, while *M. asterias* is ovoviviparous and the young develop within an egg membrane in the mother. Smooth hounds are found only on the south and west coasts of England and Ireland, on the continental shelf, and although sometimes common they are never abundant. The smooth hound is sometimes ironically called 'sweet William' because of its unpleasant smell.

The Spiny Sharks SQUALIDAE

The most abundant member of this family is the **spur-dog**, *Squalus acanthias* (Plate 5), which is easily identified by its dark grey upper parts with white spots and a sharp spine in front of each dorsal fin. This species grows to 120 cm (4 ft). The British rod-caught record is at 9·156 kg (20 lb 3 oz) for one caught in 1972 off the Needles, Isle of Wight.

Spur-dogs are shoaling fish and they are

sometimes caught in enormous numbers, all of the same sex and of about the same size. They eat herring, sandeels, cod, haddock, whiting and other gadids, and any other fish available.

The spur-dog is found all round the British Isles and is the commonest dogfish in Scottish waters. It is found at all depths on the continental shelf.

The breeding habits are well known. The females grow to a larger size than the males and are ovoviviparous. The eggs have large yolks and are in a thin membrane. About four develop together. The membrane breaks down and the young grow to about 20–33 cm (8–13 in.), at which length they are born.

Enormous numbers of this species are caught and sold in fish markets. Together with other dogfish, they are sold as 'rock salmon' after they have been skinned. The spines are particularly sharp and can inflict a wound that takes a long time to heal.

The **Greenland shark**, *Somniosus microcephalus* (Plate 6), is one of the few sharks with a predominantly northern distribution which extends from North America round south Greenland and Iceland to Norway. It grows to the large size of over 6 m (20 ft). It is dark brown or grey above, and lighter below. There are no spines in front of the dorsal fin and no anal fin.

The food of the Greenland shark consists of dogfish, cod, haddock, catfish, hake, torsk, halibut and any other available species. Very little indeed is known about its breeding.

The **bramble shark**, *Echinorhinus brucus*, is a rare southern species taken in trawls and on long lines in the North Sea, English Channel and off the Irish coasts. It can be recognized by its two dorsal fins set together near the tail, and by the skin which has scattered sharp tubercles. The **darkie charlie**, *Dalatias licha*, is caught by deep sea trawlers west of Scotland but is rarely landed. It has a large spiracle and thick lips.

Oxynotus paradoxus in the related family Oxynotidae has lateral ridges which give it a triangular body section. The first dorsal fin has a spine and is very large. Although a deep-water species, it is sometimes caught inshore.

The Monkfishes   SQUATINIDAE

The **monkfish**, *Squatina squatina* (Plate 7), is the only British member of this family. In shape it is intermediate between the round dog-fish and the flat skates. The head is broad. In relation to the head, the tail is thinner than in dogfish, but compared with skates and rays the tail is very thick. The pectoral fins are enlarged and flattened, but not to the extent found in skates. The monkfish grows to a large size 185 cm (6 ft) in length and 32 kg (70 lb) in weight. The British rod-caught record is at 29·935 kg (66 lb) for one caught off Shoreham in 1965.

The skin on both sides is rough, and is a blotched sandy grey above and white below. The colouring is such that when half buried in sand the monkfish is very well camouflaged. Its food consists almost entirely of bottom-living creatures such as plaice, dabs, soles, dragonets, skate and other fish, as well as invertebrates such as crabs, shrimps and whelks.

This species is ovoviviparous and from nine to sixteen embryos are said to develop at the same time in the mother.

Although found all round the British Isles, the monkfish is commonest on the south and west coasts, and rare in the North Sea and north Scotland. It is regularly taken by Channel fishermen, but is of little commercial value. It is often caught by sea anglers.

The Electric Rays   TORPEDINIDAE

The **electric ray**, *Torpedo nobiliana*, is a most remarkable fish because it is capable of giving a considerable electric shock. The function of the electric organs, which are situated one on each side on the 'wings' (pectoral fins), is two-fold, for attack and defence. In attack, the ray darts forward and wraps its wing round the victim, and at that moment the electric discharge is made, and the prey is stunned and swallowed. It is said that the power of the shock is sufficient to knock down anyone who may tread on an electric ray in shallow water. The fish should be handled with extreme care. It grows to 150 cm (5 ft) in length. The British rod-caught record is for one of 28·008 kg (61 lb 12 oz) caught off Skerries Bank in 1972.

The flesh of the electric ray has a flabby texture. The skin is smooth, and dark brown or slate grey. The undersides are white. The disc is almost completely circular in outline. There are two dorsal fins on the relatively short tail.

The electric ray is moderately common on the south and west coasts, but rare in the North Sea.

In the rarer *T. marmorata* the spiracle is surrounded by papillae which are absent in *T. nobiliana*.

The Skates and Rays   RAJIDAE

The skates and rays are Selachians in which the body is flattened, with the mouth on the underside. The pectoral fins are greatly enlarged on either side as wings, which are fused to the sides of the head to form a large flat disc. The pelvic fins are small, and the tail is long and thin with two dorsal fins. The tail plays little part in swimming, which is performed by means of waves that pass backwards down the margins of the wings. The flattened body form makes skates and rays very well adapted to life on the sea-bed. As the mouth is on the underside and may be buried in the sand, it might be difficult to take in the water needed for respiration through the mouth, as is usual with other fish. Instead, water is taken in through the spiracle. This is a primitive first gill opening that has become lost in the more highly evolved fish. In the skates and rays it has taken on a new function and is essential to their way of life. The spiracle is behind the eye, and in a live skate it can be seen to open and shut in regular breathing movements. The water passes over the gills and out through the openings, which are on the underside of the body.

Another adaptation to their bottom-living habit is the wonderful camouflage on the upper surface. Many skate are brown or sandy coloured with marbled or spotted patterns which blend beautifully with the stony or sandy background. The eyes are on the upper surface, and raised slightly so that the fish has a good all-round field of view. This means that, with its mouth on the underside, it cannot see what it is eating. However, skates either use their sense of touch when feeding, or their sense of smell, which as we said earlier is well developed in the Selachians. When skates and rays are seen feeding in aquaria, they pounce on their food and wrap their wings over and around it before getting it to their mouths. Their habit of living on the sea-bed leads to a diet largely composed of bottom animals, particularly crustaceans such as lobsters, crabs, hermit crabs, shrimps, prawns and amphipods, ragworms, and bottom-living fish such as dragonets, young skate, flatfish, sandeels and many other species. However, skates and rays do make excursions off the bottom and will eat herrings, sprats and gadids in considerable numbers. When several hundred stomachs of the thornback ray were examined, all contained fish, which were mainly herrings, some rays containing as many as six herrings. It may be that some species of rays and skates use the bottom as a resting-place and feed mainly in mid water. The teeth of skates and rays are in the form of a mosaic composed of modified spines.

Breeding is similar in all skates and rays; they all produce horny egg-cases similar to those of the spotted dogfishes, but in the skates, the egg-cases are squarer and the corners are drawn out into fine pointed horns and not into curling tendrils. One side of the egg-case tends to be flat and the other rounded. These egg-cases are commonly found washed up on the beach and, along with those of the spotted dogfishes, are called mermaids' purses.

Different species of skates and rays are found at different depths; some prefer a sandy bottom while others live on mud. Some swim in shoals mainly of one sex and some make local migration inshore in winter.

The names 'skate' and 'ray' have caused much confusion. There are people who have tried to limit the name skate to those with dark pigmented undersides, and the name ray to those with white bellies. Others have tried to limit skate to the long-nosed species, and ray to the short-nosed ones. This is probably the best division, and fortunately those with short noses do tend to have white bellies, and many of the long-nosed species are dark beneath. The trouble stems from the practice of calling whichever species is locally commonest, the skate. In southern England this happens to be a long-nosed species; in western Scotland it is a short-nosed one.

In recent years several deep-water species have been caught on long lines set off the continental shelf south-west of Britain, but only twelve skates are common enough in Britain to be considered here.

The Long-Nosed Skates

The **common skate**, *Raja batis* (Plate 8), is the most abundant long-nosed species and is probably the commonest skate in southern England; it is found over a wide depth range. The snout is long and the front margin of the disc is concave. The upper surface has a smooth skin with patches of prickles, but has no large spines. The colour is slate blue-grey with lighter and black spots. The underside is a dirty slate grey.

This species grows to over 210 cm (7 ft) and 180 kg (400 lb). The females are usually larger

47

than the males. The British rod-caught record is 102·733 kg (226½ lb), this specimen being caught at Duny Voe, Shetland, in 1970.

The common skate is an important commercial species and is landed in large numbers by deep-sea trawlers. Its food consists mainly of fish such as small skates, flatfish, gurnards, dragonets, mackerel and gadids, but some crustacea are also eaten.

The **shagreen skate**, *Raja fullonica*, has rather a patchy distribution. It is not found in the southern North Sea, eastern English Channel or in the Irish Sea, and it prefers moderately deep water over 35 m (20 fathoms).

The shagreen skate is a light brown or grey on the upper surface, and white below. The nose is not very long and the front margin of the disc is convex. The tail has two rows of large spines. The upper surface is covered with prickles.

The **long-nosed skate**, *Raja oxyrinchus*, is a large deep water species growing to about 150 cm (5 ft). It has a very concave anterior margin to the disc and a long nose. The skin on the dorsal side is smooth, greyish or dark brown, and without any prickles. The underside is black or greyish with dots, streaks and prickles.

The **white skate**, *Raja alba*, is a southern species whose range extends to south-west England and Ireland. The snout is pointed and the wings also extend to a sharp angle. The grey upper surface, apart from a central bare patch, is covered with prickles. The underside

is white and also prickly. The white skate grows
to 240 cm (8 ft). The rod-caught record is at
34.471 kg (76 lb).

The Short-Nosed Rays

The **thornback ray**, *Raja clavata* (Plate 9), is
probably the most abundant species, particularly
in the north, and in inshore waters. It is
sometimes known as the roker, and is called the
skate in Scotland. The colour of the dorsal
surface is a mottled greyish brown with small
black spots and larger fawn or cream-coloured
ones. The back is covered all over with
prickles and spines. There is a row of large
hooked spines down the tail (Handle with care!).
The thornback ray grows to a length of about 90
cm (3 ft). The British rod-caught record is 17·235
kg (38 lb) for one caught in 1935 at Rustington.

Female thornbacks tend to move inshore in
winter to lay their eggs, which are typical skate
mermaids' purses $7·5 \times 6$ cm wide ($3 \times 2\frac{1}{2}$ in.).

The main food of the thornback is crustacea,
e.g. hermit crabs, shrimps and swimming crabs.
Fish such as sandeels, herrings, flatfish and some
gadids are also eaten.

The thornback is the most important commercial species and contributes most to the total
British catch of skates and rays. This amounted
to 8800 tons in 1972, and was worth over £1¼
million.

The **undulate ray**, *Raja undulata*, is a southern

species that comes as far north as southern Ireland and into the English Channel. In south-western Ireland it is locally quite common. The name refers to the wavy front margin of the disc. The pectoral fins are rounded, and the upper surface is grey, fawn or brown, with an irregular pattern of broad dark stripes edged with white spots. The underside is smooth and white. The undulate ray grows to 106 cm (42 in.). The British rod-caught record stands at 8·811 kg (19 lb 6 oz 13 dm) for one caught off Herm (Channel Isles) in 1970.

The **cuckoo ray**, *Raja naevus*, has very rounded wings with a circular black and yellow marbled spot in the middle of each wing. The colour of the disc, which is covered with small prickles, is light or greyish brown. The tail is very spiny. The cuckoo ray is common all round Britain, but is rarer on the south-east coasts. It grows to 70 cm (28 in.). The British rod-caught record of 2·268 kg (5 lb) is for one caught in 1968 off the Isle of Arran.

The **starry ray**, *Raja radiata*, is a northern species extending from Iceland and Norway into the northern North Sea and the Minch. The disc is rounded, and has prickles and very large round-based spines. The upper surface is light brown marked with cream and dark spots. The underside is white. The starry ray grows to 75 cm (30 in.).

The **sandy ray**, *Raja circularis*, also has rounded wings but lacks the large spots in the centre of each wing. It is a deep-sea species found on sandy bottoms. The upper surface, which is covered with prickles, is a light sandy brown with a few creamy spots. The underside is white. The sandy ray grows to 120 cm (4 ft) and is uncommon except in deep water. The rod-caught record is at 2·565 kg (5 lb 10½ oz) for one caught off Gourock in 1969.

The **spotted ray**, *Raja montagui*, is spotted with black on a light brown dorsal surface, but the spots do not go right to the margins of the disc. The skin is smooth and without many prickles. It is a very beautiful and common ray, though absent from the northern North Sea. It grows to 75 cm (30 in.) in length. The British rod-caught record is for one of 7·342 kg (16 lb 3 oz) from Lerwick (Shetland) in 1970.

The **painted ray**, *Raja microocellata*, is found only off southern Ireland, south Wales, Devon and Cornwall. It can be identified by its grey-ish colour on the back, with white lines of irregular width which tend to run parallel to the anterior and posterior margins of the disc. The posterior half of the disc is smooth and the anterior half is prickly. This ray grows to 82 cm (32 in.). The British rod-caught record specimen was 7·37 kg (16¼ lb), caught in 1973 at Salcombe.

The **blonde**, *Raja brachyura*, is another beautifully spotted ray, but in this species the dark spots extend right to the margins of the light brown upper surface. The spots are smaller and more numerous than in the spotted ray, and also there are prickles over the upper surface. The under surface is white. The blonde is a common species on sandy bottoms in 20 to 100 m (10–55 fathoms) particularly off the south and west coasts of Britain. Like *R. montagui* it is absent from the northern North Sea. It grows to 106 cm (42 in.) in length. The British rod-caught record for this species is 17·222 kg (37¾ lb) for one caught off Start Point in 1973.

The Sting Rays   DASYATIDAE

Most species in this group are tropical, but one species, the **sting ray**, *Dasyatis pastinaca* (Plate 10), is found fairly regularly all round Britain and as far north as Bergen. This fish has a very poisonous sting, the venom being produced at the base of a spine on the top of the tail. The spine has a groove running down it, and when the fish is caught it lashes about with its tail and not only inflicts gashes with the spine, but causes paralysis and even death with the venom. It is best to stun the fish and then cut off the tail as soon as possible. A victim's wound should be made to bleed, and a temporary tourniquet fastened above the gash, which should be well washed out with sea water, and if possible dressed with a solution of potassium permanganate.

The sting ray can be distinguished from an

ordinary skate or ray not only by the spine, but also by the lack of dorsal fins on the tail. The upper surface is greyish, greenish or brown. It is a regular summer visitor in the south of England and southern North Sea, where it may be very plentiful on sandy ground. The British rod-caught record stands at 26·760 kg (59 lb) for a sting ray caught at Clacton in 1952.

The Eagle Rays   MYLIOBATIDAE

The **eagle ray**, *Myliobatis aquila*, has a longer and more whip-like tail than the sting ray, and it also has a venomous spine which is close behind a single dorsal fin near the base of the tail. The wings are sharply pointed and can grow to a spread of over 100 cm (40 in.). The total length can reach 200 cm (6½ ft). The eagle ray is a not uncommon visitor to southern England. In 1972 a record specimen of 23·813 kg (52½ lb) was caught off the Isle of Wight.

The Rabbit-Fishes   CHIMAERIDAE

The Chimaeras, which belong to the Sub-Class Holocephali, are bizarre-looking fishes with a large head, tapering body and long rat-like tail, and fins near the base. They have a smooth skin and there is one gill opening on each side and a series of mucus-secreting canals on the head. The first dorsal fin has one strong spine. The only common British **rabbit-fish** is *Chimaera monstrosa*, which is normally found on the edge of the continental shelf, but sometimes moves inshore and is caught on the deep-water trawling grounds. In 1966 one was caught in the middle of the North Sea, in unusually shallow water.

Class *PISCES*

The **sturgeon**, *Acipenser sturio* (Plate 12), is a rare British fish which is mainly of interest to students of fish evolution because it belongs to a group of primitive fishes, called the Chondrostei, whose remains are abundant in rocks laid down 300 million years ago.

The sturgeon enters the rivers Gironde in France and Guadalquivir in Spain, and Lake Ladoga in Russia, as well as the rivers of the Caspian and Azov Seas, but it is a rare fish around Britain, and probably less than half a dozen are caught each year. Sturgeon are large fish and grow to over 335 cm (11 ft) and 320 kg (700 lb). The body is elongated and has five rows of bony plates; these are half embedded in the skin and bluntly pointed, and have a texture of ivory. The snout is long and low with four barbels on the lower jaw. The backbone and flesh run into the upper lobe of the tail as in sharks and dogfish.

Sturgeon enter fresh water to breed, and in Russia there is an important industry based on them. Caviare is made from the female roe and isinglass from the swim-bladder. Isinglass is a fish gelatin used for clarifying wine and beer, for pickling and as a preservative.

The Herring Family

The herring family contains two groups, the shads which migrate from the sea to fresh water to breed, and another group containing the herring, pilchard, sprat and anchovy, which live and breed in the sea.

In both groups the fish have a single dorsal fin and no lateral line, and are covered with scales. They are all pelagic species, that is, they swim in the water layers between the bottom and the surface.

In the shads there is a distinct notch in the upper jaw which is absent from the other species, and the gill-cover has many radiating ridges. There are two shad species, and although both are rare, they are commonest on the southern and western coasts of Britain.

The **allis shad**, *Alosa alosa* (Plate 12), grows to 60 cm (2 ft) or even 76 cm (30 in.) and 3·6 kg (8 lb). The **twaite shad**, *Alosa fallax* (Plate 16), is usually 30–40 cm (12–16 in.) and rarely exceeds 50 cm (20 in.). Both species have bottle-green or greenish blue upper parts and silvery sides and bellies, with a golden iridescence particularly about the head. The twaite shad has a row of 5 to 16 large dark spots down each side and 40 to 60 gill rakers, while the allis shad has only one or two spots at the edge of the gill-cover, and 80 to 130 gill rakers. These gill rakers are like spines, and they prevent the minute drifting animals called plankton, on which the shads feed, from escaping over the gills. At one time it was thought that all the fish of the herring family swam along with the mouth open and sieved out all the food in the water. Now it is known that each individual bit of plankton is eaten separately and the gill rakers prevent its escape.

The herring, sprat and pilchard are outwardly very similar species and are often difficult to distinguish, except by their size.

The **pilchard**, *Sardina pilchardus* (Plate 11), has larger scales than the other two species; there are only about thirty scales in a direct row from the gill-cover to the tail, and there are radiating ridges on the gill-cover. The dorsal fin starts in front of the level of the pelvic fins; the belly is smooth. This fish can grow to 35 cm (14 in.) but is more often about 20 cm (8 in.). The back is greenish and the sides are silvery. Although it may be found round most of Britain, the pilchard is a southern species. It is particularly common off France and Spain, but shoals enter the Channel in summer.

Pilchards spawn in the Channel over a long period, from April to August, in different places. The eggs and larvae drift in the surface currents. Like the other Clupeids, the pilchard is a plank-tonic feeder, but it fasts from November to March. Young pilchards are caught in enormous numbers off France, Portugal and Spain, and are canned in olive oil as sardines. British pilchards are caught in the English Channel, but they do not constitute a very large fishery. Only

2150 tons were caught in 1972. Some of the catches are canned but most are exported to Italy. Since the fishery depends on the vagaries of the summer shoals, it is rather erratic.

The **sprat**, *Sprattus sprattus* (Plate 11), is the smallest member of the family and rarely grows larger than 15 cm (6 in.). It is very similar indeed to a small herring, but can be distinguished by its row of saw-toothed scales forming a keel along the belly. The front of the dorsal fin is slightly behind the vertical from the pelvic fins, but since in the herring the dorsal fin and pelvic fins are in line, and the belly is also keeled but less strongly, these characteristics are most useful if both species are present together and can be compared. The relative sizes of the jaws may be used to confirm the identification. In the sprat it does not extend behind the front of the pupil, whereas in the herring the jaw extends to the posterior edge of the pupil.

The sprat is blue, or greenish blue, above and silvery on the sides and belly. The food of the sprat is entirely planktonic and consists mainly of copepods and other small crustacea.

Sprats are found inshore round Britain but are not evenly distributed. They give rise to local coastal fisheries because where sprats are found the shoals are often very large. Over 60,000 tons were landed in 1972. Canned sprats are called brisling.

Sprats spawn in late spring and the eggs, unlike those of the herring, float in the plankton. The larvae drift inshore and the young sprats stay in shallow water and join up with young herrings. They are very tolerant of fresh water and will even move into rivers. The mixed shoals are caught and are called whitebait, which is considered a great delicacy.

The **herring**, *Clupea harengus* (Plate 13), is one of the most important food fishes caught by British fishermen. Because of this commercial importance, a great deal of research has been done into its life history and the fishery. The landings at British ports in 1972 totalled 154,400 tons and were worth nearly £5¾ million.

The back of the herring is blue, or greenish blue, and the sides and belly are silvery. The herring can be distinguished from the pilchard by the position of the dorsal fin. In the pilchard the fin starts much closer to the snout than the tail, but it is about equidistant in the herring and sprat. The differences between the herring and sprat are described under the latter species. Herrings of 43 cm (17 in.) have been recorded, but the usual length is 30–35 cm (12–14 in.). The British rod-caught record is for a herring of 481 g (1 lb 1 oz), caught off Bexhill on Sea in 1973.

The fortunes of the herring fisheries have waxed and waned. In medieval times an enormous thriving fishery existed in the Baltic, but between 1416 and 1425 it crashed, and the huge shoals dwindled to almost nothing. At the same time the North Sea fishery developed dramatically, particularly on the initiative of the Dutch. The huge English drift-net fishery, which was once based on East Anglia, has now dwindled to nothing. The timing of the different North Sea fisheries has for centuries been a progression down the east coast from the Scottish fishery in June to that off East Anglia in late autumn. It has been known for a long time that these different fisheries have been based on separate shoals, and as fishing methods have improved, it has been very important to find out to what extent the shoals represent unconnected races of herrings. If one race were to be over exploited, would the other races suffer? Numerous distinct races have been found which differ in the location of their spawning grounds, the time of year of spawning, the number of vertebrae in their backbones, the number of fin rays, scales and gill rakers of the parents, and the number of eggs they lay, as well as differences in the otoliths and other anatomical features.

There are two main groups of herrings round Britain. The Oceanic Group extends from northern Norway to the south-western coasts of the British Isles. These herrings mostly spawn in winter and spring, and they migrate huge distances over deep water between their spawning and feeding-grounds. They have a relatively long life span of up to twenty-five years and they grow to a large size (up to 37 cm; 14½ in.). They lay relatively few eggs, but these are large. The average number of vertebrae is more than 57. Examples of races in this group are the Clyde and the southern Irish herrings off Dunmore, and also those from Iceland and Norway.

The second group consists of the Shelf herrings. These inhabit the shallow water of the North Sea, the Channel and the Irish Sea. They spawn mainly in the summer and autumn on coastal banks, and they do not make extensive migrations. Their life span is of 12 to 16 years and they seldom exceed 32 cm ($12\frac{1}{2}$ in.) in length. They lay more and smaller eggs than the Oceanic herrings, and the average number of vertebrae is less than 57. Examples of this group are the herrings of the Channel and southern North Sea, those of the northern North Sea (which are a different stock) and the Minch, Isle of Man and the Baltic.

These different races of herrings spawn at different times so that somewhere or other round Britain herrings will spawn every month from July to April. The eggs sink to the bottom and stick to sand, gravel and broken shells, often in a continuous carpet of up to eight eggs thick. This demersal habit of herring eggs is in marked contrast to sprat and pilchard eggs, which, like those of all other commercially important species, are planktonic. After hatching in a few weeks the larvae, which are 6–8 mm (about $\frac{1}{4}$ in.) long, drift inshore and begin to feed on microscopic planktonic plants. As they grow larger, they turn to planktonic crustacea for food, particularly the group called copepods. These minute creatures, which are selected one at a time, are oily and make the herring very nutritious and give it its fine flavour. The young herrings collect in shoals and enter large estuaries such as the Thames; they are found in the Wash, and close to the German and Danish coasts. After six months in the coastal water they take to the open sea, but do not join the shoals of large herrings until they mature at three, four or five years of age.

The growth rate of herrings varies considerably between the different stocks and also during different years. Average figures for the southern North Sea race indicate that they reach 12 cm (4¾ in.) at one year old, 18·5 cm (7¼ in.) at two, 24·4 cm (9¾ in.) at three, 26 cm (10¼ in.) at four, and 30 cm (12 in.) at nine years of age. The maximum length to which herrings grow also varies from one race to another. For example, the Dunmore herrings grow to 29 or 30 cm (nearly 12 in.), while those off the Norwegian coast have a maximum length of 37 cm (14½ in.).

One feeding-ground for immature herrings is to the east and south-east of the Dogger Bank. Here they are subjected to another fishery by fast trawlers. At this stage they are used for making fish meal for cattle cake and poultry food. This industrial fishery has greatly reduced some of the North Sea stocks, and what once appeared to be an inexhaustible population has dwindled to almost nothing. The herrings can supply good food for men in Europe, but not for their livestock as well.

The **anchovy**, *Engraulis encrasicolus* (Plate 11), can be distinguished from other clupeids by its pointed snout and large jaw which extends back beyond the eye. The upper jaw projects considerably in front of the lower. It is a silvery fish of up to 21·5 cm (8½ in.).

The normal range of the anchovy is from the Mediterranean to the Bay of Biscay, but it is often common in the Channel, southern North Sea and Irish Sea. Instead of laying spherical eggs like most other fish, the pelagic eggs of the anchovy are oval. Spawning often occurs in estuaries where the salinity is slightly reduced.

The Salmon Family   SALMONIDAE

Most of the members of this family, which includes salmon, trout and char, breed in fresh water and go to the sea to feed. Others spend all their lives in fresh water. It is not known for certain whether the ancestral salmonid was a freshwater fish, some of whose descendants went to the richer feeding in the sea for the main part of their growing period, or whether it was a marine ancestor whose descendants found safer spawning and nursery grounds in fresh water. There is slightly more evidence for the latter view, particularly as there are other families in the group Isospondyli to which the salmonids belong that are entirely marine.

The **salmon**, *Salmo salar* (Plate 17), spends its first two, or even up to four, years in fresh water until it is about 16 cm (6¼ in.) long, when it becomes silvery and is called a smolt. It then migrates from the freshwater spawning streams to marine feeding grounds.

Until a few years ago the life of salmon in the sea was a complete mystery. Although many salmon migrating back from the feeding grounds to the spawning rivers had been caught in nets set near the coast, only a very few had been caught in deep water by commercial fishermen. Where the salmon went to feed was quite unknown. However, in 1965 a commercial fishery based on adult feeding salmon developed off west Greenland. Some of these salmon have come from British rivers and would, if not caught, return to the river of their birth. Some salmon return to breed after little more than a year at sea and these are called grilse. None of the Greenland fish are ones that would return as grilse— they have already spent too long at sea or have been back to spawn before. Where the younger fish feed is not yet known and until their feeding-grounds are discovered it is unlikely that the salmon can, like whales, be overfished almost to extinction. The food of the west Greenland salmon consists of krill (shrimp-like planktonic crustacea), herrings, sandeels, and caplin (an arctic smelt).

The salmon at sea is a magnificent fish; the back is a silvery blue-green, the flanks are silvery and the belly is white. Scattered over the flanks are small round and X-shaped spots. All the members of this family have a small fleshy, adipose fin.

The **sea trout**, *Salmo trutta* (Plate 20), is superficially very like a small salmon. The back is a bluish grey, the flanks silvery and the belly is white with dark round and X-shaped spots. In the salmon all the spots are usually above the lateral line; in the sea trout some are below and there are nearly always a few red spots. Other differences are in the length of the upper jawbone, which in the salmon reaches to the eye, and in the trout extends to behind the eye. In the sea trout the region just in front of the tail (the 'caudal peduncle') is thick, while in the salmon it is relatively thinner and makes a convenient hand hold. In spite of these differences, and others in the detailed scale counts, the sea trout and salmon are often confused.

The sea trout is less marine in its habit than the salmon and probably remains for most of its life in the vicinity of the coast. At one time the sea trout was thought to be a different species from the brown trout of fresh water, but now they are both thought to be variations of one extremely variable species. An intermediate form is the slob trout which drops down from fresh water to brackish estuarine conditions. Some of these fish take on the sea trout's silvery colour, but

others remain similar to a typical freshwater
trout.

The Smelts OSMERIDAE

The **smelt**, *Osmerus eperlanus* (Plate 16), like the
salmonids, has a fleshy adipose fin between the
dorsal and tail fins. Also like the salmon and sea
trout, it lives in the sea and enters fresh water
to spawn. Adult smelt are usually about 20
cm (8 in.) in length, though very occasionally
they may become double that size. The body
is slender; the smelt has a large mouth with a
protruding lower jaw, and large teeth. The
lateral line does not extend far down each side
from the head.

The upper parts are a greenish or grey-green,
the sides silvery and the belly white. The skin
of living smelts has a semi-transparent appearance. A characteristic feature of this fish is a
distinct smell of cucumbers.

Smelt are mainly estuarine and coastal fish.
In Britain they are found on the east coast from
Kent to the Forth, and on the Lancashire coast.
In Ireland they are reported from the Shannon
estuary. Smelt enter rivers to spawn in March.
The yellowish eggs are sticky and adhere to
rocks, tree stumps, piles and similar objects.

They are deliciously flavoured fish with white
flesh.

The Argentines ARGENTINIDAE

The **Argentine** or **silver smelt**, *Argentina sphyraena*, is a frail little fish of about 28 cm (11 in.) with a translucent body and a broad silver stripe down each side. The adipose fin is colourless. Argentines are commonest in depths of 90 to 200 m (25–110 fathoms) off the northern and western coasts of Britain.

The Eel ANGUILLIDAE

Eels are unlikely to be confused with any other fish, except perhaps the lampreys, from which they can be immediately distinguished by their pair of pectoral fins. Eels are very well known and their slipperiness is proverbial. They can live a long time out of water and have a remarkable tenacity of life. The body of an eel is long and cylindrical, and only laterally flattened towards the tail. These fish have no ventral fins, and the dorsal, tail and anal fins are joined. The gill slits are small and the scales, set in a very slimy skin, are minute.

Apart from rare stragglers from further south, only two species of eel (in two families) are found around Britain. The best known is the **common eel**, *Anguilla anguilla* (Plate 1), which migrates into fresh water and is probably present in every pond, ditch and canal. It is a very tough creature and can withstand more pollution and bad living conditions than any other British fish. The common eel breeds in the sea in the area of the Sargasso Sea between Bermuda and the Leeward Islands. The adults die after breeding, but the eggs and larvae float in the surface currents, particularly the North Atlantic Drift which slowly crosses to Europe. The young eels, called *leptocephalus* larvae, are shaped like a laurel leaf. They start at about 5 mm in length and after about three years, when they reach Europe, they are 7·5 cm (3 in.) in length. They metamorphose (change shape) to completely transparent glass eels 6·5 cm (2½ in.) in length. These move inshore and become pigmented, when they are called elvers. The elvers move into fresh water in thousands during March, April and May, but many remain in the sea, particularly frequenting rocky shores, jetties and pier piles, where there is mud to bury in or weed to hide in. It has been suggested that the females go inland and the males remain in the sea, but this is not entirely true. When the males are about 40 cm (16 in.), after about nine years, and the females are nearing 60 cm (24 in.), after about twelve years, they become silvery and migrate to the sea.

Eels in the sea feed on crabs, shrimps, prawns, worms, molluscs, young fish and other bottom animals. In general, however, very little is known about their life and habits in the sea.

The **conger eel**, *Conger conger* (Plate 21), is
entirely marine. The lower jaw, which is
shorter than the upper, and the pointed rather
than rounded pectoral fin, which almost reaches
the commencement of the dorsal, are characteristics which distinguish the conger from the
common eel. Also the eye is larger and elliptical
in the conger and rounder in the common eel.

The conger is brown above and dirty white
below on the belly; larger specimens from muddy
or deep water are purplish or grey above. The
conger eel grows to a much larger size than the
common eel. The males can reach 80 cm
(31 in.) but are usually smaller. Females are
often 120 to 150 cm (4–5 ft), but specimens of
240 cm (8 ft) and 58 kg (128 lb), and 270 cm
(9 ft) and 73 kg (160 lb) are on record. The
British rod-caught record is for a conger of
43·401 kg (95 lb 11 oz) caught off Brixham in
1973.

Small congers are sometimes found on rocky
shores between tide marks, but they are more
often below low tide mark among rocks, jetties,
pier piles, harbour walls and wrecks. They are
distributed all around Britain but are less common on the east coast.

European conger eels spawn between Gibraltar
and the Azores, in about 3000 m (1600 fathoms).
The eggs float in the sea, not on the surface, but
at a great depth. The young pass through

leptocephalus, glass eel and elver stages, but little is known of the details of the early life history and growth rates.

The diet of the conger is mainly fish and a very large variety of species is eaten, including shore fish, flatfish, herrings and dogfish. Some crabs, lobsters, squids and cuttlefish are also eaten.

The **moray eel**, *Muraena helena* (which is dark brown marbled, blotched and spotted with yellow), has occasionally been reported from Cornwall.

The Garfishes BELONIDAE

The **garfish**, *Belone bellone* (Plate 14), is like a very large sandeel 60 to 75 cm (24–30 in.) long, with finely pointed jaws extending forward like the bill of a snipe. Both jaws have many very sharp teeth. The long dorsal and anal fins are set far back and extend nearly to the forked tail. The pelvic fins are midway along the body. The upper parts are bright blue-green and the sides are silvery. The scales are rather small. The fins are dark, except for the yellowish pelvics and anal. The only fish with which the garfish could easily be confused is the saury pike described next, and the differences are given there.

The garfish is not common except in summer and autumn when it moves northwards to south-west Britain, but it does not often enter the North Sea. It is a fish of the upper layers of the ocean, though when it comes inshore it will penetrate even into estuaries. It appears to shoal with mackerel, and has often been taken with them in drift-nets in the western Channel.

The garfish is said to be very good to eat, and it is an interesting fish to have served because the bones, even when cooked, are an unusual turquoise green. It is obviously helpful to have a fish in which the bones are clearly visible.

Spawning takes place inshore. The large eggs are peculiar in that they have long filaments with which they become entangled with one another and with weed. The lower jaw grows first, and not until the fish is 5 cm (2 in.) in length does the upper jaw begin to elongate.

Garfish are not caught commercially, but are often taken by anglers, and the rod-caught record stands at 1·282 kg (2 lb 13 oz 2 dm) for one caught off Newton Ferrers in 1971.

The Saury Pike   SCOMBERESOCIDAE

The **saury pike**, *Scomberesox saurus* (Plate 14), is very similar to the garfish but is less elongated and has shorter upper and lower jaws with finer teeth. The best distinguishing feature is that in the saury pike the dorsal and anal fins are split into a main portion and a series of separate finlets near the tail.

The saury pike rarely exceeds 46 cm (18 in.) and is therefore smaller than the garfish. **In** colouring the two species are very similar, though the saury pike has a bright silver streak down the side.

The saury pike is an oceanic fish which shoals near the surface. Those that are found around the shores of Britain are ones that have taken part in an annual northerly migration from their usual haunts farther south. They have a habit of leaping out of the water and scuttering over the surface, perhaps while escaping from predators. In this way they resemble the flying fish, to which they are related.

The Pipefishes   SYNGNATHIDAE

This family contains some of the most interesting and charming British fish. They are mainly residents of inshore weed beds—particularly the eel-grass *Zostera*. One species, the sea-horse, is very well known, but the others are not so familiar to the layman.

The pipefishes are very elongate fish in which the head is drawn out into a long snout. The tail is also long and in some species does not have a caudal fin. In all the species there is a complex bony skeleton of plates and rings which gives an angular appearance.

The pipefishes have one feature which is almost unique in the animal kingdom; the eggs are brooded in a special pouch by the male and not by the female. The different stages in the evolution of the pouch in which the male incubates the eggs can be seen in the British species. In the genus *Entelurus* the belly of the male is rounded and the eggs are stuck to it in rows. In the genus *Nerophis* there is a shallow groove in which the eggs lie. In *Syngnathus* there is even more protection for the eggs, as the edges of the groove have grown up as two flaps that come together in the mid line over them. This means that the eggs lie in a brood pouch which is only open along a median slit. In the sea-horse *Hippocampus*, the two flaps are joined and there is only one small opening into the brood pouch. The male and female intertwine and the eggs are fertilized as they are laid into the brood pouch.

The fins of the pipefishes are very much reduced. The pectoral fins are small and the anal fin is minute. The pectoral fins, and in some species the tail fin also, are missing. The pipefish are very slow moving and propel themselves with a rapid beating of the dorsal fins. Mostly they live among seaweeds without moving far.

The food of all the species consists almost entirely of tiny crustaceans which are stalked with great care and deliberation. The prey have to be minute because the mouth, situated at the end of the long snout, is very small.

One of the commonest species is the **great pipefish**, *Syngnathus acus* (Plate 15), which grows to 46 cm (18 in.) in length. It has pectoral, dorsal and anal fins, and a well-developed tail fin. The snout is long. The profile over the head is markedly humped. It is most fre-

73

quent among seaweeds and eel-grass *Zostera*. The **broad-nosed pipefish**, *Syngnathus typhle* (Plate 15), has a more whip-like tail and a much smoother profile over the eye. It is less common, and at 30 cm (12 in.), is smaller. A fairly common species is the **lesser pipefish**, *Syngnathus rostellatus*. The snout is relatively short and slender, and there is a hump over the eye. The body rings and ridges are conspicuous. This species is found on sandy shores in 60–200 cm (2 ft to 6½ ft) of water, just below low tide mark, particularly among seaweed.

The **snake pipefish**, *Entelurus aequoreus* (Plate 15), has no pectoral or anal fins. There are minute tail fin rays, but not a tail fin such as in the *Syngnathus* species. The snout is long and slender with a smooth profile over the eye. This species seems to come into British coastal waters from the Atlantic, where it appears to live an oceanic existence.

The *Nerophis* pipefishes have no tail, anal or pectoral fins. The **worm pipefish**, *Nerophis lumbriciformis* (Plate 15), is the commonest pipefish between tidemarks, where it may be found under boulders or among seaweed hold-fasts. It has a very short snout and grows to 15 cm (6 in.). It is widely distributed and common on rocky coasts. The **straight-nosed pipefish**, *Nerophis ophidion* (Plate 15), is mainly sublittoral among seaweeds. It has a long snout with a straight profile over the eye. It grows to 25 cm (10 in.).

The **sea-horse**, *Hippocampus ramulosus* (Plate 15), is a rare visitor to Britain from the Bay of Biscay. It is too well known to need a detailed description. It is a fascinating creature to watch. When the sea-horse swims it keeps an upright position, moving in a jerky manner by means of its dorsal fin. More often it is seen quite motionless with its prehensile tail wrapped round the stem of a seaweed.

The Cod Family   GADIDAE

This large family includes such familiar and economically important species as the cod, haddock, whiting and hake. The haddock in particular has a very good flavour indeed, particularly if absolutely fresh. Other species, for example the Norway pout and the rocklings, are completely unknown to the layman. While some British species go as far south as subtropical waters, most are fish of the arctic North Atlantic. Some species are oceanic and others are found intertidally, but the greatest number of species are in moderate depths on the continental shelf. Only the burbot, is found in fresh water.

All the gadidae have soft fin rays and smooth scales which are sometimes small and occasionally fairly large. Some have barbels on the upper lip and many have one or more barbels on the chin. The family can be divided into three groups depending on the fin arrangements.

In one group there is a single long dorsal fin and a similar anal fin, e.g. the torsk. In another group there is a single long anal fin, but the dorsal is divided into two, the first of which is smaller, e.g. the hake, ling and rocklings. In the third group there are two anal and three dorsal fins; this group contains the cod, haddock and whiting. In the rocklings the first dorsal fin is modified into a chemical sensory organ with a single whip-like first ray, and a row of short hair-like rays set in a groove which is in continuous motion, driving water over a chemical taste organ.

All the marine species have eggs which float in the plankton and also planktonic larvae, and as a consequence they are widely distributed.

The **cod**, *Gadus morhua* (Plate 24), is the best known and one of the most numerous members of the family. It is a favourite quarry of sea anglers and is very important commercially. Nearly 318,500 tons, worth over £49¾ million, were landed in 1972 in British ports. These figures are higher than for any other species.

The cod is recognizable by having three dorsal fins and two anal, and having greenish or reddish mottled upper parts and a white lateral line. It has a single barbel on the chin. The cod grows to over 160 cm (5¼ ft) in length and 40 kg (88 lb in weight). The British rod-caught record stands at 24·039 kg (53 lb) for a cod caught off Start Point, Devon, in 1972.

There are numerous races of cod which have their own centres of distribution and annual migrations to feeding and spawning grounds. For example, one stock inhabits the North Sea and another the area between Spitzbergen, Bear Island and northern Norway. Although there is probably some interchange between the stocks, their significance lies in the probability that without some care, they will be overfished, and recovery might be slow.

Cod spawn in the North Sea over the Great Fisher and Ling Banks from January to April. The floating eggs take about twelve days to hatch. Starting at 4 mm, the larvae feed chiefly on drifting planktonic animals called copepods until about two months, at 2 cm (¾ in.), they take to the bottom, where they eat small bottom-living crustacea such as shrimps and little crabs. They remain bottom-feeding fish for the rest of their lives and commonly consume *Nephrops* (scampi), crabs, hermit crabs, marine worms and brittle stars. As they grow larger they eat fish, and the prey consists of herring, sandeels and haddock, as well as their own kind. In the North Sea they reach 18 cm (7 in.) in their first year, 36 cm (14 in.) in their second, 55 cm (22 in.) in their third, until they are 89 cm (35 in.) in their sixth year. They do not begin to breed until they are five years old and 70 cm (27 in.) in length, though they are liable to be caught in trawls at one and a half to two years of age and 30 to 35 cm (12 to 14 in.) in length. There are obvious overfishing dangers when a species can be caught before it has had a chance to breed.

77

Commercially the **haddock**, *Melanogrammus aeglefinus* (Plate 24), is the second most important member of the gadid family. The catch in 1972 was 155,500 tons, and as haddock is also expensive, this catch was worth £21 million. Besides having an excellent flavour when fresh, the haddock is also delicious cured. It is not as often caught by anglers as is the cod, but nevertheless is much sought after. The British rod-caught record is for a haddock of 4·876 kg (10 lb 12 oz) caught in 1972 off Looe in Cornwall.

The haddock is recognized by its three dorsal and two anal fins, its brownish olive back and silvery sides and belly, by its black lateral line and a dark black spot on each side between the base of the pectoral fin and the lateral line. This is said to be the thumb-print of St Peter when he picked the haddock out of the sea. The haddock has a small barbel on the chin.

In the North Sea the haddock spawns from about February to April. The females are not as prolific as those of the cod. The eggs, which are slightly larger than the cod's, float in the surface water. The larvae hatch in about two weeks, and they too are planktonic. In some years very few of the larvae survive, but in other years there is very good survival. Although various ideas have been put forward to account for this, such as that the wind direction influences survival, the cause of brood fluctuations is not yet known. It is certain, however, that the number of young fish available to be caught each year is not directly connected with the number of spawning adults that gave rise to them. Whatever the cause of the brood fluctuations, the result is that after a good year the haddock is remarkably plentiful in the catches, and one good year-class may dominate the landings until it is fished out completely. The haddock reaches 17 cm (7 in.) at one year, 30 cm (12 in.) at two and 80 cm (31 in.) at ten years.

The food of the haddock consists almost entirely of bottom invertebrates such as worms, brittle stars, bivalve molluscs and snails, and also large quantities of herring spawn at the right season.

The haddock is a northern species and is uncommon in the southern North Sea and the Channel. It is found northwards as far as Trondheim in Norway, and westwards to Iceland, Greenland and the Newfoundland Banks. It is commonest between 40 and 300 m (20–160 fathoms).

The **whiting**, *Merlangius merlangus* (Plate 26), is another very important commercially caught member of the cod family. In 1972, 36,950 tons, worth £3,879,000, were landed at British ports. Really fresh whiting has a delicate flavour, but this is soon lost.

The whiting is a more slender fish than the cod or haddock. It has three dorsal and two anal fins; the lower jaw is shorter than the upper, and there is no barbel on the chin. The upper parts are a golden olive green, and the sides and belly are silvery with a golden sheen. The lateral line is thin and brown. There is a black spot at the base of the pectoral fin, but this cannot easily be confused with the larger and more definite thumb-print of the haddock which is above the fin base.

Spawning in the whiting takes place mainly in March and April in around 100 m (55 fathoms). The newly hatched whiting is about 3·4 mm long and by the time it is 25 mm (1 in.) long the adult characteristics have appeared, and it has a barbel. This disappears when the whiting reaches 5 cm (2 in.) in length. Small whiting of 3 cm (1¼ in.) are very common inshore and they are frequently found associated with jellyfish, which are often the stinging kinds. The little whiting swim in small shoals just in front of the jellyfish and dart into the protection of the tentacles when danger threatens. They reach 17 cm (6½ in.) in their first year, 25 cm (10 in.) in their second, and become mature in their second spring.

Whiting tend to swim in shoals either in midwater, or just off the bottom over sand or sandy mud in 50 to 150 m (25–80 fathoms).

The whiting is more a mid-water feeder than the cod or haddock. Very small whiting feed on minute plankton and crustacea larvae, and move on to large plankton such as krill, and shrimps, as they grow bigger. They also eat prawns, small crabs, amphipods, gobies and sandeels. Large whiting eat many species of fish such as small herrings, sprats, whiting, Norway pout and sandeels.

The **saithe**, *Pollachius virens* (Plate 22), is sometimes called the coal fish on account of its dark bottle-green, blue or brown upper parts. The belly is a dull silver. There are three dorsal and two anal fins, a minute barbel on the chin which is absent on large specimens, and a very slightly protruding lower jaw. The lateral line, which is light coloured, is straight or only slightly curved. Over 47,000 tons of saithe, valued at over £3 million, were landed in British ports in 1972, so it is of moderate commercial importance, but the value is not sufficient for it to be a fish specially sought after by commercial fishermen; rather it is a fish caught incidentally while seeking more valuable species.

The saithe is commonest in northern inshore waters and the young ones are often abundant round Hebridean piers and the tangles off rocky shores. The older, larger specimens of up to 100 cm (40 in.) are caught further offshore. The British rod-caught record is at 13·947 kg (30 lb 12 oz) for a fish caught off Eddystone Lighthouse in 1973.

Saithe spawn in February and March off north-west Britain and in the northern North Sea. The young grow quickly to about 25 cm (10 in.) in the first year.

Saithe are shoaling fish and they feed in mid-water on planktonic crustacea when they are small, and on fishes, such as sandeels, gobies, herrings and young gadids, when they are older.

The **pollack** or **lythe**, *Pollachius pollachius*

(Plate 26), is superficially like the saithe, but can be distinguished because the lower jaw protrudes beyond the upper, and the lateral line has a distinct curve over the pectoral fin. Another characteristic which aids identification is the colour, which is usually more of a muddy brown or green than the dark green or blue of the saithe, and the lateral line is dark.

Pollack are not important commercially but are very popular with sea anglers. The British rod-caught record is 11·339 kg (25 lb) for a pollack caught off Eddystone Lighthouse in 1972. They grow to a length of 130 cm (50 in.).

The pollack has a more southerly distribution than the saithe, and although their ranges overlap considerably, they tend to replace each other as common fish, with the saithe in the north and pollack in the south. Pollack are found mainly on rocky ground near reefs and headlands. They shoal less than saithe, except at spawning time.

Pollack spawn in March or April, but little is known about the life history of the young. Growth is rapid and at the end of their second summer they range from about 20 cm (8 in.); after four summers they are about 40 cm (15¾ in.).

The food of the pollack is taken in mid water and consists of planktonic crustacea and fish such as sandeels, herring, pilchard, sprats, wrasses, gobies and some flatfish and young gadids.

The **bib**, or **pout** as it is sometimes called,

Trisopterus luscus (Plate 19), is a deep-bodied gadid. It has three dorsal and two anal fins. The first anal fin is long. It has a conspicuous barbel on the chin.

The upper parts of the bib are a beautiful coppery bronze with darker vertical bands. The lateral line is a brown seam which curves over the pectoral fin. There is a black spot at the base of the pectoral fin.

The bib grows to 40 cm (16 in.) in length, though the more usual size is 30 cm (12 in.). The bib is often caught by anglers and the British rod-caught record is 2·494 kg (5½ lb) for one that was caught in 1969 off Berry Head.

The bib is one of the British gadids with the most southerly distribution. It is found in the western Mediterranean and off Spain, and although it has been recorded from all round Britain, it is commonest in the south and west.

Spawning takes place mainly in March and April in 35 to 100 m (20–55 fathoms). The eggs hatch in ten to twelve days and the fry are found inshore among weed. After one year they reach 20–25 cm (8–10 in.) and about 30 cm (12 in.) in their third year.

The food of the bib is mostly bottom invertebrates such as shrimps and prawns, crabs, hermit crabs, polychaete worms and some fish.

The **poor cod**, *Trisopterus minutus* (Plate 19), is another gadid which is found in the Mediterranean (but is a different race) and is found all round Britain. Superficially the poor cod is similar to the bib, but although it also has three dorsal and two anal fins, and a distinct barbel on the chin, it is less deep bodied. In the bib the pelvic fin reaches beyond the vent to overlap the anal fin, but in the poor cod it reaches only to the vent.

The coloration of the poor cod is a brownish or yellowish brown on the upper parts. The sides are a silvery brown. There is a small dark spot at the base of the pectoral fins.

The poor cod is smaller than the bib. It rarely exceeds 23 cm (9 in.). A poor cod of 283 g (10 oz) caught off Gourock in 1970 holds the British rod-caught record. The poor cod is a more offshore fish than the bib, though spawning in March and April occurs in 50–100 m (25–55 fathoms). Only the young fish during their first and second years are found close inshore.

The diet is composed of bottom-living animals such as shrimps, gobies, dragonets, gurnards, worms, swimming crabs, squat lobsters and other bottom crustacea.

The **Norway pout**, *Trisopterus esmarkii*, is distinguished from the bib and poor cod by its smaller size and lower jaw which is longer than the upper. It has a small barbel, three dorsal and two anal fins. It grows to 23 cm (9 in.) but is rare above 20 cm (8 in.). The colour of the upper parts is brown-bronze with silvery sides. Its food consists of copepods, crustacea and krill.

The Norway pout is found in abundance off

northern Britain in deep water of 100–200 m
(55–110 fathoms), but it is rarely seen inshore.
It is economically important because it is a common item in the diet of cod, hake, ling and
whiting. It is also caught in mid-water trawls
for conversion into fish meal.

The next group of the species in the family
Gadidae are those with two dorsal fins and one
long anal fin. The first species described here
is the **hake**, *Merluccius merluccius* (Plate 18).
Some authorities place the hake in a separate
family, the Merluccidae, on account of the arrangement of its long sharp teeth and projections
on the vertebrae over the body cavity. These
projections form a strong roof over the swim-
bladder. Here we will group it with the gadids.

The hake is a deep-water fish found mainly in
150 to 550 m (80–300 fathoms), but because it has
an excellent flavour it is often seen on the fishmonger's slab. It has a large head with a big
mouth, the inside of which is black; and has sharp
teeth. The body is slate blue or grey above with
silvery sides and belly; the lateral line is black.
The hake grows to over a metre in length. One
of 11·495 kg (25 lb 5½ oz) caught in Belfast Lough
in 1962 holds the British rod-caught record.

The hake feeds by night in mid water, where
it is caught on long lines, but by day it retires to
the bottom where it is caught by trawlers. The
migrations from the bottom in deep water to
near the surface involve great changes in pressure,
and if the hake is to remain so that it neither

floats nor sinks, considerable changes have to be made in the amount of gas in the swim-bladder, and the bladder itself has to withstand relatively large changes in pressure. The bony projections from the vertebrae, and the muscles attached to them, are probably connected with the ability to withstand these pressure changes. The migration off the bottom at night to feed is so regular that the trawlers do not bother to put their nets down in the evening, but wait until daylight. The food of small hake consists of krill, and large hake feed entirely on squid and fish such as whiting, Norway pout, small hake, mackerel, herring and the blue whiting, *Poutassou*.

The hake spawns late in the season, in July, off the Hebrides and off south-west Ireland. The survival of a particular brood depends on the drift of the young to shallow inshore nursery grounds. In years when the winds are predominantly easterly, the developing eggs and the planktonic larvae are driven out into the Atlantic and the survival that year is very poor.

The main hake ports in Britain are Fleetwood in Lancashire and Milford Haven in South Wales. The British landings in 1972 amounted to 2500 tons, worth £758,000.

The **ling**, *Molva molva* (Plate 28) has a slight resemblance to the hake in that it is a large fish with two dorsal fins and one long anal fin. However the ling grows to a much larger size, and may be 200 cm ($6\frac{1}{2}$ ft) in length. The British rod-caught record ling was 22·906 kg

($50\frac{1}{2}$ lb) in weight and was caught off the Eddystone Lighthouse in 1974.

The upper parts of the ling are grey, brown or bronze-green. The flanks and dorsal surface may have light or dark marbling patterns, or a few scattered blotches or spots. The dorsal and anal fins have white edges, with a dark border inside the white edge on the anal and second dorsal fins. Small ling, above 7 cm (3 in.), have an olive-brown band along each side with lighter bands above and below. At about 18 cm (7 in.) these bold longitudinal stripes break up and turn into the drab marbling of the adults. The ling is a thinner fish than the hake, and it has a conspicuous barbel.

Ling are usually considered deep-water fish and are often found down to 400 m (220 fathoms), but they also occur in shallower water of 40 m (22 fathoms). They are said to frequent rocky ground and old wrecks, and they are found from Brittany to northern Norway and Iceland.

Ling breed from April to June in about 200 m (110 fathoms) and a fair-sized female is said to lay up to 60 million eggs in one season. The large-sized females may be up to fourteen years of age. The growth of the young is rapid at first. They reach 20 cm (8 in.) in their first year and 33 cm (13 in.) in their second.

The diet of the ling is composed almost entirely of fish, particularly cod, Norway pout and other gadids, as well as herring, mackerel, gurnards, dogfish and flatfish. Some squids are also eaten,

87

and it is said that salmon has been found in their stomachs.

Many people, particularly in Scotland, consider ling is very good to eat, and it is often salted and cured. It is a fairly valuable commercial species and is caught on long lines and in trawls. The British landings in 1972 were 4600 tons, worth £504,000.

The **blue ling**, *Molva dypterygia* (Plate 28), is a similar species with a northern distribution. It differs from the ling in having its lower jaw longer than the upper, in being a uniform coppery colour without any markings, and in having a longer narrow body. It is a deep-water species found at 350 to 500 m (190–270 fathoms) off northern Britain, Iceland and Norway. It is often landed by commercial fishing boats.

Another fish of deep water, but in this case with a distribution centred to the south of Britain, is the **greater fork-beard**, *Phycis blennoides* (Plate 18). It is usually found at 150 to 300 m (80–160 fathoms), though it often strays into shallow water of 10 m (5 fathoms), particularly when young. The main centre of distribution is from the western Mediterranean to the west coast of Britain, but this species is rarer off the Scottish coasts.

The chief characteristic feature of the greater fork-beard is the pelvic fins which are far forward under the gills; each has two long filamentous rays which extend back to the anal fin. The fish has two dorsal fins and one anal, and a barbel on

the chin. The scales are large and easily de-
tached. The general colour of the upper parts
is brownish, shading lighter below. The dorsal,
tail and anal fins are edged with black.

This species is of little commercial importance
and is not often caught by anglers, though there
is a British rod-caught record for one of 2·133 kg
(4 lb 11¼ oz) caught in Falmouth Bay in 1969.
The greater fork-beard is said to be poorly
flavoured, and does not compare with the hake
with which it is often caught.

The **lesser fork-beard** or **tadpole-fish**,
Raniceps raninus, is a very different looking
creature (Plate 47). Tadpole-fish is the better
name for it as it is tadpole shaped. It has a small
barbel and the first dorsal fin is reduced to one
ray. The scales are small and inconspicuous in
the uniformly dark brown skin. The mouth and
lips are noticeably light. It grows to 25 or
30 cm (10–12 in.). One of 403 g (14¼ oz) caught
in Seaham Harbour holds the British rod-caught
record.

The lesser fork-beard is a northern fish which
is found most commonly from Wales and East
Anglia to Norway. Young specimens come
inshore and, in Scotland, are sometimes caught
in lobster creels. It is of no commercial importance.

The rocklings are a group within the family
Gadidae with several characteristics which set
them apart from the others. They are all elongate fish with a single anal fin and two dorsal fins,

the first of which is modified into a special sense organ. This first fin consists of one long fin ray followed by a row of very short hair-like rays set in a shallow groove. The short rays are in a constant vibratory motion, and waves of movement can be seen passing backwards down the row. These waves draw a small current of water over what is believed to be a chemical sensory organ which, so to speak, 'tastes' the water ahead of the fish.

The identification of rocklings is helped by the different number of barbels on the different species. Most confusion has been caused in the past over the two species with three barbels. The first of these is the **shore rockling**, *Gaidropsarus mediterraneus*. This species has two barbels on the upper lip and one on the chin. The small mouth extends only a little way, if at all, beyond the eye. Its colour, which is a uniform dark brown, is also an aid to identification. The shore rockling is distributed in Britain mainly in the south and west, in the Irish Sea, off southern Ireland and western Scotland. It is most commonly found in rock pools, among boulders and seaweed intertidally, but it also occurs just sublittorally. It grows to 25 cm (10 in.). The British rod-caught record is at 298 g (10½ oz) for one caught off Guernsey in 1974.

The other species with three barbels, the **three-bearded rockling**, *Gaidropsarus vulgaris* (Plate 23), is a bigger species which grows to 50 cm (20 in.). It has two barbels on the upper

Sea lamprey (p. 25)
River lamprey (p. 27)
Common eel (p. 67)

Pl. 1

Basking shark (p. 36)
Thresher shark (p. 37)

Pl. 2

Blue shark (p. 38)
Smooth hound (p. 29)

Pl. 3

Porbeagle (p. 35)
Tope (p. 39)

Pl. 4

Lesser-spotted dogfish (p. 33)
Greater-spotted dogfish (p. 32)
Spur-dog (p. 40)

Pl. 5

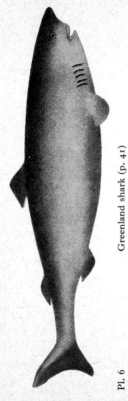

Greenland shark (p. 41)

Pl. 6

Monkfish (p. 42)

Pl. 7

Pl. 8   Common skate (p. 47)

Pl. 9   Thornback ray (p. 49)

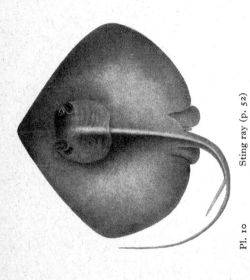

Pl. 10   Sting ray (p. 52)

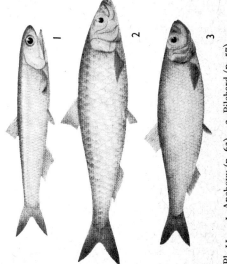

Pl. 11   1. Anchovy (p. 63).   2. Pilchard (p. 57).
3. Sprat (p. 58).

Sturgeon (p. 55)
Allis shad (p. 56)

Pl. 12

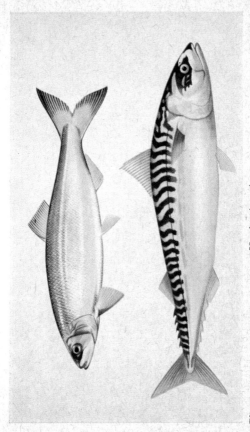

Herring (p. 59)
Mackerel (p. 116)

Pl. 13

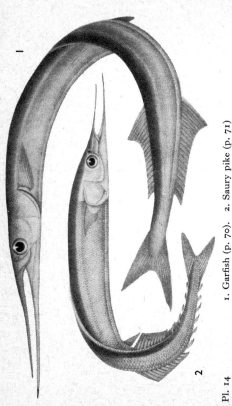

1. Garfish (p. 70).   2. Saury pike (p. 71)

Pl. 14

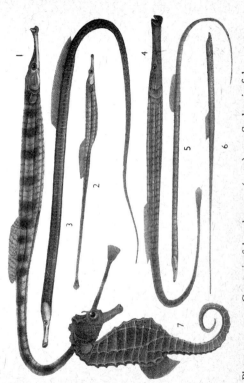

Pl. 15   1, 2. Great pipefish and young (p. 73).   3. Snake pipefish
(p. 74).   4. Broad-nosed pipefish (p. 74).   5. Straight-nosed
pipefish (p. 74).   6. Worm pipefish (p. 74).   7. Sea-horse (p. 75)

Twaite shad (p. 56)
Smelt (p. 66)

Pl. 16

Salmon, male (*above*) and female (p. 64)

Pl. 17

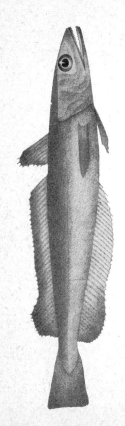

Hake (p. 85)
Greater fork-beard (p. 88)

Pl. 18

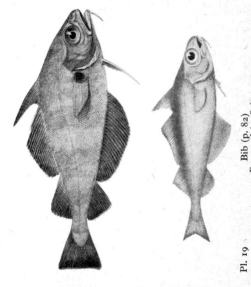

Bib (p. 82)
Poor cod (p. 83)

Pl. 19

Sea trout, male (*above*) and female (p. 65)

Pl. 20

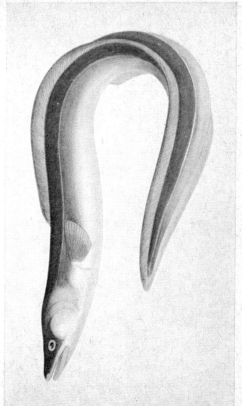

Conger eel (p. 69)

Pl. 21

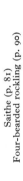

Saithe (p. 81)
Four-bearded rockling (p. 90)

Pl. 22

Three-bearded rockling (p. 90)
Five-bearded rockling (p. 91)

Pl. 23

Cod (p. 76)
Haddock (p. 78)

Pl. 24

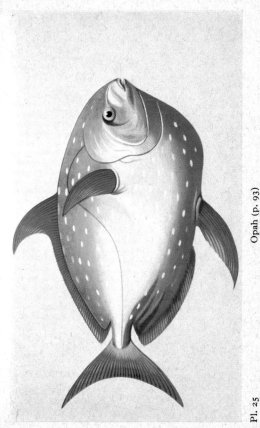

Opah (p. 93)

Pl. 25

Whiting (p. 79)
Pollack (p. 81)

Pl. 26

Pl. 27

John Dory (p. 94)
Boar-fish (p. 95)

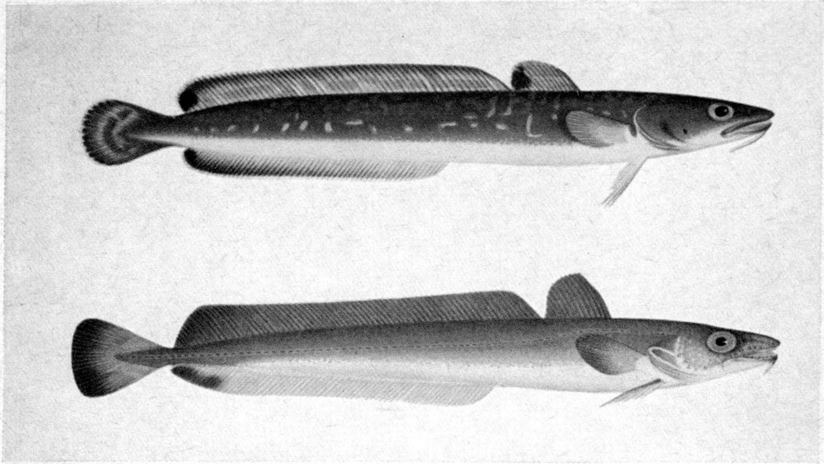

Ling (p. 86)
Blue ling (p. 88)

Pl. 28

Horse mackerel (p. 99)
Pogge (p. 147)

Pl. 29

Bass (p. 96)
Red sea bream (p. 104)

Pl. 30

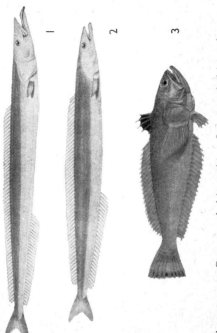

Pl. 31   1. Greater sandeel (p. 112).   2. Lesser sandeel (p. 112).
3. Lesser weever (p. 114)

Red mullet (p. 103)
Greater weever (p. 115)

Pl. 32

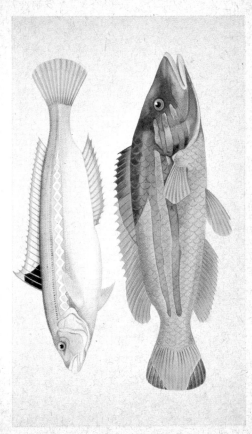

Rainbow wrasse (p. 109)
Cuckoo wrasse (p. 109)

Pl. 33

Tunny (p. 118)

Pl. 34

Pl. 35   1. Shanny (p. 129).   2. Yarrell's
blenny (p. 132).   3. Montagu's blenny (p. 130)

Corkwing (p. 111)
Ballan wrasse (p. 108)

Pl. 36

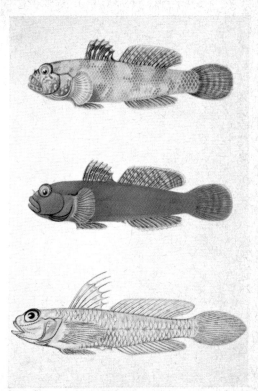

Pl. 37   Rock goby, female (p. 125)
Rock goby, male
Fries' goby (p. 125)

Butterfly blenny (p. 130)
Viviparous blenny (p. 133)

Pl. 38

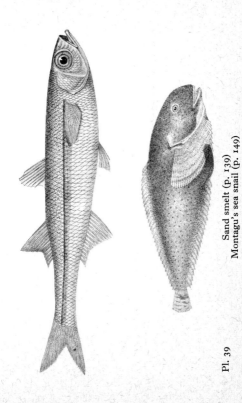

Sand smelt (p. 139)
Montagu's sea snail (p. 149)

Pl. 39

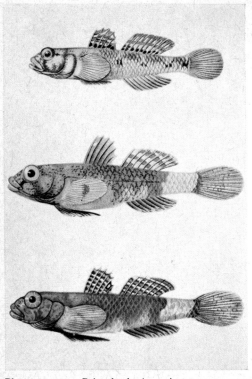

Pl. 40   Painted goby (p. 124)
Diminutive goby, female (p. 126)
Diminutive goby, male

Spotted dragonet (p. 128)
Fifteen-spined stickleback (p. 151)

Pl. 41

Tub gurnard (p. 143)
Red gurnard (p. 143)

Pl. 42

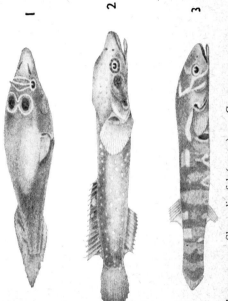

Pl. 43　　1. Shore clingfish (p. 172).　2. Connemara
clingfish (p. 173).　3. Two-spotted clingfish (p. 172)

Catfish (p. 134)
Black goby (p. 124)

Pl. 44

Butterfish (p. 131)
Red-fish (p. 140)

Pl. 45

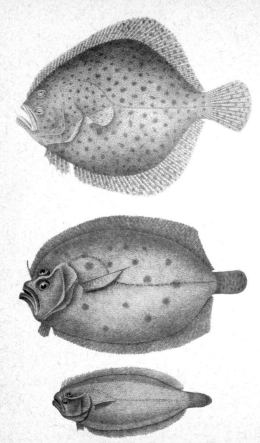

Pl. 46   Turbot (p. 153)
Bloch's topknot (p. 155)
Scaldfish (p. 157)

Grey mullet (p. 136)
Lesser fork-beard (p. 89)

Pl. 47

Common dragonet (p. 127)

Pl. 48

Streaked gurnard (p. 144)
Grey gurnard (p. 142)

Pl. 49

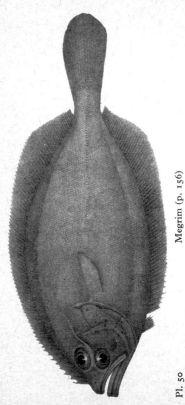

Megrim (p. 156)

Pl. 50

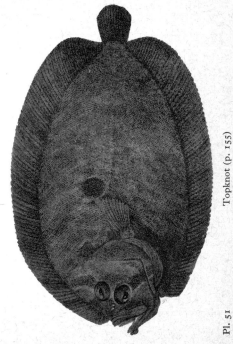

Topknot (p. 155)

Pl. 51

Pl. 52   Long-spined sea-scorpion, male (*above*) and female (p. 145)

Pl. 53   Lumpsucker, male (*above*) and female
(p. 147)

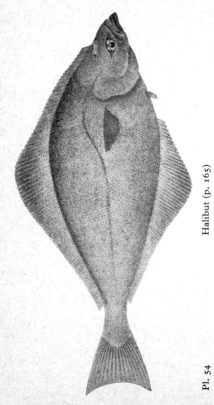

Halibut (p. 165)

Pl. 54

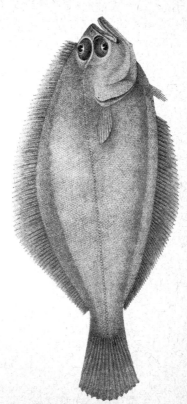

Long rough dab (p. 164)

Pl. 55

Pl. 56

Brill (p. 154)
Plaice (p. 158)

Sole (p. 166)
Sand sole (p. 168)

Pl. 57

Dab (p. 160)

Pl. 58

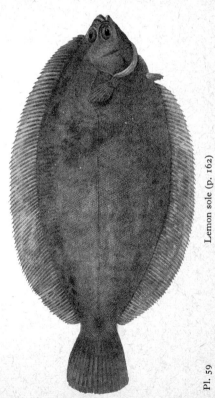

Lemon sole (p. 162)

Pl. 59

Solenette (p. 168)
Thick-back sole (p. 169)

Pl. 60

Pl. 61 Sunfish (p. 170)

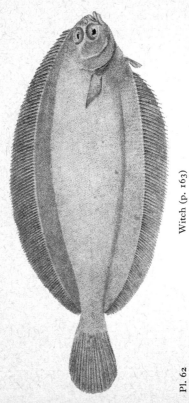

Witch (p. 163)

Pl. 62

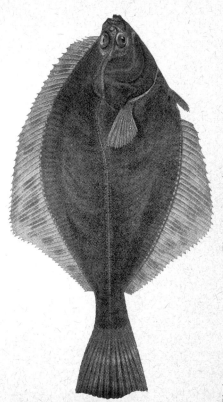

Flounder (p. 161)

Pl. 63

Angler fish (p. 173)

Pl. 64

lip and one on the chin, but its mouth is relatively larger than that of the shore rockling as it extends quite definitely well beyond the eye. The colour also is distinctive. The ground colour is yellow, brown or pinkish, and on this are broad dark brown spots, marbling and blotches, which extend from the body on to the fins. The three-bearded rockling occurs all round Britain, and is a deeper-water species than the shore rockling. It is found in 10 to 120 m (5–65 fathoms) on rocky ground. It is sometimes caught from the shore by sea anglers. The British rod-caught record is 1·311 kg (2 lb 14¼ oz) for one caught in Poole Bay in 1972.

The **four-bearded rockling**, *Rhinonemus cimbrius* (Plate 22), has two barbels by the nostrils, one on the upper lip, and one on the chin. It is a light or reddish brown colour and lighter on the sides, which shade into a dull grey on the belly. The dorsal and anal fins are dark grey with a light edge, and each has a round black spot near the tail. The four-bearded rockling is a deep-water species on soft muddy bottoms, at 50 m (27 fathoms) to 550 m (300 fathoms). It is a northern species with a range from the British Isles to Norway. It grows to 35 cm (14 in.).

The **five-bearded rockling**, *Ciliata mustela* (Plate 23), has two barbels by the nostrils, two on the upper lip, and one on the chin. The upper parts are brownish, but can be very dark if it has been living on a dark background. It has no spots or other markings.

The five-bearded rockling is common in rocky shore pools and in shallow water among weed and boulders. It is found all round Britain and from Spain to Norway. It grows to 20 cm (8 in.). The British rod-caught record of 262 g (9¼ oz) is for a five-bearded rockling caught at Lancing Beach in 1968.

The **northern rockling**, *Ciliata septentrionalis*, has probably been confused with the five-bearded rockling for a long time, because since I first found it in the Clyde area in 1960, it has been recorded from many other places. It has a row of barbels like a moustache fringing the upper lip, as well as the five barbels seen in *C. mustela*. It is usually caught offshore and must still be considered a very rare fish.

The eggs of all the rocklings are pelagic and they float in the surface waters. They are very small and have an oil globule. The three-bearded and five-bearded rocklings breed very early in the year, while the four-bearded breeds between May and August, and the shore rockling in July and August. All the rocklings have a long larval life; and the larvae have green backs and silvery sides. The larvae move inshore and are often very abundant; they are called mackerel midges. Rocklings have no commercial importance.

The last gadid to be considered is the **torsk**, *Brosme brosme*, a species with one barbel, which is on the chin. This fish differs from all other British members of the cod family by having

THER
BO RE

GE
Y.

NO.

B   BLE   ***003.95
B   NTY   ***000.32
S B   *004.27

F   001350   ***004.27

NO CASH REFUNDS

only one dorsal fin, and this and the anal fin are joined at the base to the tail fin. The colour is brown or greyish, and the unpaired fins have a black band with a white edge. The torsk grows to 100 cm (39 in.). It is found in deep water off northern Britain. Although caught commercially it has not much importance. The British rod-caught record torsk of 5·471 kg (12 lb 1 oz) was caught off Shetland in 1968.

The Opah   LAMPRIDIDAE

The **opah**, *Lampris guttatus* (Plate 25), is a truly magnificent fish. It grows to 150 cm (5 ft), and because of its globular shape, a fish of this length weighs over 50 kg (110 lb). The colour of the opah is very striking. It is blue above and red on the belly, with silvery sides and irregular oval milky white spots. The fins are scarlet.

The opah is an oceanic fish living at moderate depths over the North Atlantic, where it feeds mainly on squid and fish. It is a rare fish and most records are of stranded specimens, though some are taken on lines and in trawls. It is said to be extremely good to eat. Its other names are the moon-fish and king-fish. The British rod-caught record of 53·057 kg (128 lb) is for an opah caught in Mounts Bay in 1973.

The Deal-Fish   TRACHIPTERIDAE

The **deal-fish**, *Trachipterus arcticus*, is a deep-water species which in some years (e.g. 1966 and

1967) comes into shallow water in considerable numbers. It is a long fish with a laterally compressed body, a long dorsal fin and a tail with the ventral part missing. It grows to over 2 m (6½ ft).

The John Dory   ZEIDAE

The **John Dory**, *Zeus faber* (Plate 27), is a most extraordinary and odd-looking fish. It grows to about 50 cm (20 in.) and although the body is almost as deep as it is long (without the tail), it is extremely narrow, almost as if cut out of cardboard. The head is large, and the mouth is also large, and set at an angle which gives the fish a very miserable expression. However, the large jaws can hinge forward into a protrusible tube which is very adept at catching its prey of small fish. The dorsal fin consists of two portions: the first has nine or ten long spines, and the second has shorter rays. The anal fin has four very stout spines in front of the rest of the fin. There are sharp spines on the belly.

The prevailing colour of the body is greyish or olive-brown with a yellow metallic sheen. There is a very conspicuous black spot with a yellow halo behind the pectoral fins. This spot has given rise to the legend that the dory was caught by St Peter in the Sea of Galilee, and the black spot is supposed to be the apostle's thumb mark when he lifted the fish from the water. However, a similar legend is attached to the haddock, and neither of these fish is at all likely to have ever been in the Sea of Galilee.

The John Dory appears to be a solitary fish with very feeble swimming powers. Its food consists of gadids, small herrings, sandeels and other small fish. It is remarkably efficient at stalking its prey, which is soon within striking distance and engulfed by the protrusible mouth.

The John Dory is usually found at moderate depths of under 100 m (55 fathoms), mainly to the south and west of Britain. It is most commonly caught by trawlers working over sandy ground.

The spawning season is relatively late, from June to August. The eggs are sticky, about 2 mm in diameter, and the growth is fast so that the Dory reaches 25 cm (10 in.) in its second winter.

The dory is said to be good to eat, but it has little economic value. It is often caught by anglers and the British rod-caught record stands at 4·876 kg (10¾ lb).

The Boar-Fish   CAPROIDAE

The **boar-fish**, *Capros aper* (Plate 27), looks in many ways like a smaller, coral pink, version of the John Dory, but it has more of a snout, is less circular in outline, and is considerably less laterally flattened.

The boar-fish is mainly a deep-water fish of down to 400 m (220 fathoms) where it lives on rocky ground. It has been suggested that the large numbers that sometimes enter the English Channel, and are seen off Devon and Cornwall, have been carried from their usual habitat by surges of water upwelling along submarine canyons on the edge of the continental shelf.

The boar-fish grows to 15 cm (6 in.) and feeds mainly on planktonic crustacea. It spawns in July and has no economic value.

The Sea Perches   SERRANIDAE

The sea perches or basses, which are all marine, are related to the freshwater perches of the family Percidae. There are a great many species of sea perches, but most of them are tropical or subtropical. Only four species are recorded from the seas around Britain, though there are ten species in the Mediterranean. They all have two dorsal fins, which in most species are connected. The first fin is spiny and the second has soft-branched rays. The single anal fin has three strong spines.

The commonest British sea perch is the **bass**, *Dicentrarchus labrax* (Plate 30), which is a handsome fish and extremely popular with sea anglers.

The bass grows to 100 cm (39 in.) in length and 12 kg (26½ lb) in weight, but British specimens are smaller. The British rod-caught record is at 8·220 kg (18 lb 2 oz) for a bass caught at Felixstowe in 1943.

The back of a bass is metallic blue or greenish grey, the sides are silvery and the belly is white.

Young ones under 15 cm (6 in.) have some dark grey spots. The body is firm and covered with rough scales. The two dorsal fins are separated though close together. The first dorsal fin has eight or nine spines. The opercular and pre-opercular bones have sharp spines, so this species must be handled with care.

The food of the bass is composed of crustacea such as amphipods, isopods, small crabs and shrimps and small fish, but the large bass mainly consume fish such as sprats, herrings, sandeels, young gadids and flatfish.

The bass is found all round Britain and as far north as Stavanger in Norway, but it is mainly a southern species of warmer waters. It is most plentiful in the English Channel and off southern Ireland.

The spawning of bass has for many years been rather a mystery. Recently Irish scientists have found that bass spawn a few eggs at a time through May and early June in bays and off the mouths of estuaries, and that the eggs hatch in four or five days. According to these scientists growth is slow. After one year the fish are about 9 cm (3½ in.), and at two years old 16 cm (6½ in.). It takes about five years for a female bass to reach 450 g (1 lb), 16 to 20 years to reach 4·5 kg (10 lb) and 20 to 22 years to reach 5·5 kg (12 lb). The males grow more slowly and do not live as long as the females. Bass appear to spawn for the first time when they are five or six years old.

There is a definite inshore migration of bass

from March to May, when they enter brackish water and often move right into fresh water.

Bass seem to like places where rocks meet sand, shingle or mud, particularly round off-shore reefs. The young fry are found very close inshore in creeks and tidal pools.

The male and female bass are separate individuals, but some other species in this family, e.g. the comber, are hermaphrodite.

The three other species in this family are the **wreck fish**, *Polyprion americanus*, the **comber**, *Serranus cabrilla*, and the **dusky perch**, *Epinephelus guaza*. In these species the two dorsal fins are joined. The wreck fish is the commonest, and most often comes to British waters while accompanying drifting weed, wood or other flotsam. A comber of 467 g (1 lb ½ oz), which was caught off the Wolf Rock Lighthouse in 1972, holds the British rod-caught record. The comber is a reddish- or grey-streaked fish with dark bars across the back. Very few specimens of this, or the dusky perch, have been found round the British Isles and neither need be considered in more detail here.

The Horse Mackerels CARANGIDAE

The species in this family have compressed streamlined bodies. They are mid- or surface-water swimmers, and feed on fish. In all species there are two separate spines in front of the anal fin. In some species there are two distinct dorsal fins, but in others the first dorsal is reduced to a row of spines with no membrane between them.

There are four species recorded from British waters. The rarest is the **amberjack**, *Seriola dumerili*, which has been caught only once, by an angler at Salcombe in 1952.

The **pilot fish**, *Naucrates ductor*, is a fish of the tropical and subtropical open seas, which comes to this country with sharks or sailing boats. It has a peculiar habit of swimming just beneath sharks, turtles, boats and drifting wood. Many kinds of fish seem to like sheltering under large objects. They can probably see their prey more easily from the shade of something above them. This may explain the association of young whiting with jellyfish. The pilot fish is characterized by five to seven dark blue vertical bands on each side from the back to the belly.

The **derbio** or **glaucus**, *Trachinotus ovatus*, is another rare vagrant from warmer Atlantic waters and the Mediterranean. It is a deep-bodied fish with four to six round dark spots along the lateral line.

The commonest member of the family is the **horse mackerel**, *Trachurus trachurus* (Plate 29), also known as the scad. It is easily recognized by the row of large plate-like scales or scutes which extend along the entire length of the lateral line from the operculum to the tail, with a characteristic dip below the gap between the first and second dorsal fins. The body form is similar to that of the mackerel, but the head and eyes are larger and the body is deeper. The lower jaw protrudes beyond the upper, and the first dorsal fin is composed of eight rays connected by a membrane. There are two strong, sharp spines in front of the rest of the anal fin. The pectoral fins are long and sickle-shaped. The tail is deeply forked. The upper parts are metallic blue or olive-green, the sides are silvery and the belly is white. The gill-cover has a dark spot. There are none of the beautiful markings found on the ordinary mackerel.

The horse mackerel migrates into British waters in spring and early summer, and spawning occurs from June to August. The adults are often taken in considerable numbers by fishing boats in the southern North Sea, English Channel and the south-western approaches. However the commercial value of the horse mackerel is not very great in Britain, where the flesh is considered coarse and not particularly palatable. In southern Europe the horse mackerel is more abundant and of more economic value.

The eggs and larvae of the horse mackerel are pelagic. The young fry of about 4 cm ($1\frac{1}{2}$ in.) are often found close inshore in very large numbers, and they form mixed shoals with other kinds of fish. The food of the young horse mackerel is mainly planktonic crustacea such as copepods and euphausid shrimps. The large ones eat young herrings, sprats, pilchards and other pelagic fish.

Horse mackerel are often caught by anglers, though seldom specially sought after. The rod-caught record stands at 1·488 kg (3 lb 4½ oz) for one caught off Plymouth in 1971. The horse mackerel grows to 40 cm (16 in.).

Ray's Bream   BRAMIDAE

Apart from the rare vagrants the **long-finned bream**, *Taractes longipinnis*, and *Taractes asper*, which have both been reported twice from British waters, and *Pterycombus brama* which has been recorded only once, **Ray's bream**, *Brama brama*, is the only member of this family which comes to Britain at all regularly. All the Bramidae are mid-water fish with a wide oceanic distribution. They have deep compressed bodies and grow to a moderately large size. Ray's bream is distributed from the south Atlantic to Iceland, but is commonest to the south of Britain. There is an annual migration northwards from off Spain in the autumn and early winter. The number involved varies considerably. There was a large invasion into the North Sea in 1966, and even greater ones in 1967 and 1969.

Ray's bream grows to a length of about 65 cm (25½ in.). It has a very blunt rounded head, large mouth and eyes. The dorsal and anal fins are long and pointed, and the tail fin is deeply divided with long curved lobes. The upper parts are olive-green, the sides are silvery and the pectoral fins are yellow. Most often Ray's bream is reported from specimens washed ashore, but some are regularly taken by anglers. The British rod-caught record stands at 3·621 kg (7 lb 15¾ oz) for one caught off Hartlepool in 1967.

The Meagre SCIAENIDAE

The **meagre**, *Argyrosomus regium*, is the only British member of this tropical and subtropical family. The meagre is a large fish of up to 200 cm (6½ ft). It has a small spiny first dorsal fin and a long second dorsal fin. The anal fin is short, and this combination of fin arrangement is characteristic. The head, as well as the body, is covered with scales. The upper parts are silvery brown, and the sides and belly are silver with a golden sheen. The fins are reddish brown.

The meagre is only a rare vagrant round Britain, though odd individuals are reported fairly frequently.

Some species in the Sciaenidae have well-developed air-bladders and special muscles that they can vibrate to produce remarkable drumming or rumbling noises.

The Red Mullets

There is a difference of opinion about whether the two forms of red mullet are separate species or only varieties of one single species. There is also disagreement as to whether the smaller form which has been called *Mullus barbatus* is found as far north as the British Isles. Even if it is found round Britain, it is very much rarer than the other form called *M. surmuletus* (Plate 32). Here we need only say that one of the chief distinguishing characters of *M. barbatus*, which only grows to 20 cm (8 in.), is the lack of three yellow bands which are present in the other form. The remainder of this account will be about the **red mullet**, *Mullus surmuletus*. This fish is a brilliant red (often redder than the specimen shown in Plate 32) with scales on the back, edged with brown. There are three longitudinal bands along each side. The first of the two dorsal fins has a dark trailing edge. The snout of the red mullet is very blunt and there are two very characteristic long stiff barbels which fold back into two grooves. The tail is deeply forked. The red mullet is mainly a migrant that comes inshore on the south and south-west coasts from May to September, from warmer southern waters.

The red mullet is prized almost above all other fish by epicures, and fantastic prices have been paid for mullet since Roman times. The main fishery for this species is in the Mediterranean and it is too rare to be important in Britain. However, the red mullet is occasionally taken by trawlers and anglers. It grows to over 40 cm (16 in.). The British rod-caught record of 1·644 kg (3 lb 10 oz) is for a red mullet caught off Guernsey in 1967.

The Sea Breams   SPARIDAE

This is another family of fishes which are mainly tropical and subtropical It is an enormous family with only two common representatives in British waters, but another six are rare vagrants.

All the species are deep, laterally flattened fish with large scales even on the head. The single dorsal fin is long and made up of two portions; the first is spiny and the second has soft-branched rays. The anal fin is short and has three sharp spines. The characteristic feature of the sea breams is their teeth. These differ among the different species; in some they are sharp cutting teeth, while in others they are flat crushing teeth.

The commonest member of this family is the **red sea bream**, *Pagellus bogaraveo* (Plate 30). This species is an orange red over the head, body and fins. There is a large black spot at the beginning of the lateral line, but this may be lacking in young specimens. The front teeth are pointed and those behind are rounded crushing teeth. The anal fin is longer than in most other species.

The red sea bream is common at the western end of the Channel and off south-west Ireland in fairly deep water, but in the summer there is an annual movement up the west coast and into the North Sea, and even as far as Norway. Bream are usually found on rough, rocky ground, where they swim in shoals near the bottom.

The red sea bream is said to be hermaphrodite, but it has been suggested that only one roe, male or female, is active in any one individual fish.

The sea bream is taken by trawlers in deep water, and after the summer inshore migration it is often caught in shallower water by sea anglers. The British rod-caught record stands at 3·402 kg (7 lb 8 oz) for a red sea bream caught in 1925 off Fowey.

The **black sea bream**, *Spondyliosoma cantharus*, is the second commonest British member of the Sparidae. It has the same general compressed shape as the red sea bream, but the anal fin is shorter. The teeth are sharp and pointed, and it is presumably with these that the black bream obtains its food, which is said to consist of encrusting algae and animals on rocks, as well as a few free-swimming creatures.

This species is dark blue-grey or black above, with silvery-grey sides that have a metallic sheen. There are often horizontal golden brown streaks, and six or seven dark vertical bands on the sides. However, the coloration is very variable and changes with age.

The black bream is commonest in the south

and west, and is very local in its occurrences. It is rare round the north of Britain and in the North Sea. There is an annual migration to the eastern end of the Channel, where considerable numbers congregate. The British rod-caught record of 2·941 kg (6 lb 7¾ oz) is for one caught off the Eastern Blackstone Rocks, Devon, in 1973.

Of the six rarer species, the **bogue**, *Boops boops*, is a rare wanderer to the north of Britain, but occurs fairly frequently in the southern North Sea, English Channel and southern Ireland. The teeth of the bogue are flattened notched incisors, in a single row in each jaw. The body is longer and thinner than in other sea breams. The colour is an olive-blue with three to five yellow stripes. The British rod-caught record bogue weighed 733 g (1 lb 9 oz 14 dm) and was caught off Jersey in 1968.

The **pandora**, *Pagellus erythrinus*, is only occasionally reported from south-west Ireland and Cornwall, and is a very rare vagrant else-where. It is similar to the red sea bream, but lacks the red spot and has a relatively much smaller eye.

The **gilt-head**, *Sparus aurata*, has been re-corded infrequently along the Channel coasts and very rarely elsewhere. There are three strong pointed canine teeth on each side of each jaw. Its name derives from a golden band between the small eyes. The upper parts are blue-grey or greenish purple, and the belly is silvery. One of 1·523 kg (3 lb 5¾ oz) was caught off Alderney,

Channel Isles, in 1973 and holds the British rod-caught record.

Of the remaining three rare species, the **Spanish bream**, *Pagellus acarne*, has a conspicuous black spot at the base of the pectoral fin, and has only occasionally been reported from Devon, Cornwall and the Firth of Forth.   The **dentex**, *Dentex dentex*, has been recorded about seven times, and the **pagre**, *Pagrus pagrus*, twice from British waters.

The Red Band-fish   CEPOLIDAE

The **red band-fish**, *Cepola rubescens*, is immediately recognizable by its long, thin, bright red or orange-red compressed body, with dorsal and anal fins, and a small head with a large mouth.   This species lives in burrows in sand or mud.   It lives off the south and west coasts, and occasionally is carried inshore in large numbers. It grows to 70 cm (27 in.) in length. In 1972 a record specimen of 74 g (2 oz 10 dm) was caught at Portland Harbour.

The Wrasses   LABRIDAE

There are seven species of British wrasses, though many more are found in warmer southern waters. The British species are common inshore fish of no commercial value.   They have thick lips and strong teeth.   Some of the species have brilliant colours, though the smaller ones are more drab.

In some wrasses there are also differences in the colours of the two sexes; the males are usually much more brilliantly coloured than the females.

The food of the wrasses is mainly molluscs, crustacea and barnacles. All these hard-shelled creatures are first bitten by the strong front teeth, and later crushed by special grinding 'pharyngeal' teeth in the throat. Most of the wrasses are inshore fish which frequent rocky and seaweed-covered areas.

All the wrasses have a single long dorsal fin, the first half of which is composed of sharp spines; the posterior portion has soft branched rays. The anal fin is relatively short, and in most species has three sharp spines anterior to the soft rays.

In two common species, the corkwing and rock cook, and in the rarer scale-rayed wrasse, the pre-operculum is serrated and in the others it is smooth. The pre-operculum is the flat bone lying in front of the gill-cover.

The **ballan wrasse**, *Labrus bergylta* (Plate 36), is a large, rather elongate species with a small mouth and large lips. The scales are large and conspicuous. The pre-operculum is smooth. The body has an irregular variegated pattern of small blotches of brown, red and green. The fins are reddish with white spots. The ballan wrasse builds a loose nest of seaweed, bound together with mucus, in which the sticky eggs are laid. The larvae have a short planktonic stage before moving close inshore. The ballan wrasse lives near the shore and feeds on barnacles and tube worms which are scraped off the rocks, as well as on crabs and molluscs. Although found all round Britain, it is commonest on the west coasts. It grows to over 50 cm (20 in.). The British rod-caught record specimen of 3·485 kg (7 lb 10 oz 15 dm) was caught in 1970 off Cornwall.

The **cuckoo wrasse**, *Labrus mixtus* (Plate 33), is the most elongate British wrasse and has a large mouth and thick lips. The pre-operculum is usually smooth. The colour of the male is often very brilliant. His head and back are royal blue, which extends as dark lines on each side to the tail. The back of his body is red, turning to bright yellow on the belly. The female is a uniform red above and silver below, with three dorsal black spots near the tail, and another at the front of the dorsal fin.

The cuckoo wrasse is commonest on the west coast, but has been found all round the British Isles. It is more often caught offshore than are any of the other British wrasses. Little is known about its biology, but it grows to 35 cm (14 in.). The British rod-caught record cuckoo wrasse from off Plymouth in 1973 weighed 949 g (2 lb $\frac{1}{2}$ oz).

The **rainbow wrasse**, *Coris julis* (Plate 33), has brilliant but very variable coloration. It has sharp, protruding teeth, and a black spot at the front of the dorsal fin. The male has a yellow or orange zig-zag pattern down each side on top of a purple band, and this has green above it and silver below. There are dark and light bands on the dorsal and anal fins. In the female there is a brown band with blue above and silver below. Apart from its colours, a distinctive feature of the rainbow wrasse is the absence of scales on the head and gill-covers. It grows to 25 cm (10 in.), and is a very rare fish, most commonly reported from southern England.

Another rare and easily identified wrasse is the **scale-rayed wrasse**, *Acantholabrus palloni*, the only British wrasse in which the scales extend on to the dorsal, caudal and anal fins. It has been reported only twice, each time from Cornwall.

The remaining three species are dumpy wrasses living inshore and rarely exceeding 15 cm (6 in.) in length.

The **rock cook**, *Centrolabrus exoletus*, is distinguished by having four or more anal fin spines and serrations on the pre-operculum that continue from the hind edge on to the lower margin. This fish is greenish brown with blue spots on the fins. Most individuals grow to 15 cm (6 in.).

In the **goldsinny**, *Ctenolabrus rupestris*, which also may have four anal spines, the pre-opercular serrations do not extend from the hind margin to the lower border. The body is brownish orange with two distinctive black spots, one at the anterior end of the dorsal fin, and the other in front of the tail on the dorsal surface. It is found on rocky shores among seaweed, and in intertidal pools, and is commoner on the south and west coasts than in the North Sea. Its food is believed to consist mainly of small crustacea and molluscs.

The **corkwing**, *Crenilabrus melops* (Plate 36), is the commonest small inshore wrasse of rocky coasts and shore pools all round Britain. It rarely if ever has more than three anal fin spines, and the serrations on the pre-operculum extend from the hind margin to the lower edge. There is a black spot on each side below the lateral line, in front of the tail. The body has orange or brown markings on an olive background. The corkwing rarely grows above 18 cm (7 in.). The British rod-caught record specimen of 283 g (10 oz) was caught at Langland Bay in 1974.

The food of the corkwing consists of barnacles, tube worms and small crustacea, snails and bivalves. This species makes a nest in which the eggs are laid.

The Sandeels   AMMODYTIDAE

Sandeels are long silvery fish which, although very active and adept at escaping capture, are not as sinuous and flexible as the true eels. They have a hard skin, a single dorsal fin and a long anal fin. There are no pelvic fins. All the species are silvery. Some species frequent the open sea and others are found buried in sand between tide marks. Until recently only two species were thought to be present round Britain, but now five are known to be fairly common. Some species are extremely abundant and of great importance economically because they form a vital link in the food chain from plankton to commercial fish such as cod, haddock and herring. Not only do they form the food of fishes, but also of guillemots, puffins, razorbills and other sea birds. As well as their importance as a food for edible species of fish, sandeels are caught in considerable numbers in a commercial fishery for fish meal and cattle-cake manufacture.

Of the inshore species, the **lesser sandeel** *Ammodytes tobianus* (Plate 31), can be distinguished by having a protrusible jaw which can shoot out to form a tube; this is very suitable for catching planktonic food. The dorsal fin starts in front of the line from the tip of the pectoral fin. The lesser sandeel is found in abundance round Britain, buried in sand between tide marks or swimming in shallow water. The eggs are laid in the sand to which they stick. The young are planktonic and get distributed widely. The lesser sandeel grows to 20 cm (8 in.).

In the other inshore species the dorsal fin commences posterior to the tip of the pectoral fin. The first of these is the **greater sandeel**, *Hyperoplus lanceolatus* (Plate 31). The jaw is not protrusible, and there is a black spot on the side of the snout in front of the eye. The back is bluish green and the sides and underparts are silvery. It grows to 33 cm (13 in.). A record sandeel of 70 g (2½ oz) was caught off Anglesey in 1973.

The greater sandeel tends to inhabit deeper water than the lesser sandeel, but nevertheless can be found intertidally on sandy beaches near low tide mark. It is distributed all round Britain. The eggs are laid in deep water and the larvae are planktonic.

A similar and rarer species is *H. immaculatus*, which can be distinguished from the greater sandeel by the absence of the black spot on the snout. It is found off Cornwall, south-western Ireland and western Scotland.

Of the offshore species, **Raitt's sandeel**, *Ammodytes marinus* (the young of which are also found inter-tidally) is the most numerous. It is important as a food for other fish. Raitt's sandeel is very similar to the lesser sandeel, from which it is distinguished by irregularly arranged rows of scales on the belly, and by not having scales on the lobes of the tail. The back is greenish blue, and the sides and belly are silvery. It grows to about 25 cm (10 in.). It is plentiful round Britain, Norway and Iceland. In the North Sea it feeds principally on worms, small crustacea and fish eggs and larvae.

Another offshore species is the **smooth sandeel**, *Gymnammodytes semisquamatus*. This can be distinguished by its lateral line which has small branches at right angles to the main canal. It is browner than the other sandeels. It is found most commonly on the west coasts and less frequently in the northern North Sea.

The Weevers TRACHINIDAE

This family contains the only common poisonous British fishes. They must be treated with very great care because the poison causes considerable pain, and to susceptible people, real illness. Recommended treatments are to bathe the wound with potassium permanganate or with very hot water.

The commoner and most venomous species is the **lesser weever**, *Trachinus vipera* (Plate 31). The poison is in glands at the base of the first dorsal spine, and the spine on the operculum (gill-cover). These spines are grooved, and when they are pressed the poison is driven up the groove. Weevers often lie half buried in sand, so it is very easy for the unwary paddler to tread on the fish, and the poison shoots up into the foot. Similarly, it is very easy to pick up a weever inadvertently when sorting through a catch of shrimps mixed up with seaweed and flotsam.

The lesser weever is a stumpy, blunt-headed fish with a large mouth that is inclined upwards. The eyes are large and on the top of the head. There are two dorsal fins (the first of which has the poison spine) and one long anal fin. The back is yellowish brown with darker brown markings and the belly is lighter. The first dorsal fin is black.

The lesser weever is found all round the British Isles, though more commonly in the south. It lies in the sand near low tide mark and below, with only its eyes and poisonous spines exposed. Here it waits on its prey of small shrimps and other crustacea. It grows to 10 or 15 cm (4–6 in.).

The **greater weever**, *Trachinus draco* (Plate 32), is a species of deeper water and so is most harmful to trawlermen and other offshore fishermen. The body of the greater weever is more elongate than that of the lesser species, and it has small spines below each eye. It is dark grey with yellowish sides and dark markings that run obliquely downwards with the scale rows. The first dorsal fin has a black spot on the membrane between the first two or three spines, and the long second dorsal and anal fins have a yellow stripe.

Like its smaller relative, the greater weever is a bottom-living fish which lies buried in the sand. Its food consists of small crabs, shrimps and bottom-living fish. It grows to 40 cm (16 in.), and is found all round the British Isles. The British rod-caught record greater weever was caught at Brighton in 1927 and weighed 1·020 kg (2¼ lb).

Both weevers spawn from June to August; the eggs are small (1·0 mm in diameter in the greater, and up to 1·4 mm in the lesser weever) and they float in the plankton.

The Mackerel Family   Scombridae

The mackerel family, which includes the tunnies and bonitos, consists of well-streamlined and powerful swimming fish. They form a group which is unlikely to be confused with any other. They have smooth torpedo-shaped bodies with two dorsal fins, the second of which (and the anal fin) degenerates posteriorly into a series of small finlets. Most of the members of this family are oceanic fish that inhabit the surface waters of temperate and tropical oceans. They are fast and graceful swimmers and make large migrations. Sometimes these migrations seem to get a little off course and bring rare southern species to the British Isles.

Apart from these, however, there are two common species on British coasts, particularly during the summer. All the members of the family, from the humble mackerel to the 800-lb tunny, are good sport fish. They are all beautifully coloured, blue or green above and silvery below, and they are very good to eat and highly nutritious.

The best known, and one of the smallest, is the **mackerel**, *Scomber scombrus* (Plate 13). The back is blue or green with dark blue-black wavy lines, and the sides and belly are silvery. Mackerel grow to 55 cm (22 in.) and the rod-caught record is 2·452 kg (5 lb 6½ oz) for one caught north of the Eddystone Lighthouse in 1969.

The migrations of the mackerel have been the

subject of prolonged research. In June and July the large spawning shoals break up into small shoals which move inshore and feed voraciously on young herring, sprats, sandeels and other small fish. They remain in the bays round the coasts through summer and autumn until November, when they leave the shallow surface waters. At this time they begin to collect in compact concentrations in hollows and pits in the sea floor. Towards the end of the year these concentrations begin to spread out over the sea-bed, and the mackerel feed on shrimps, amphipods, worms and small fish, and other bottom-living creatures. About February they rise towards the surface and form new shoals which slowly migrate to the spawning areas. One spawning area, where mackerel from the Channel, western France, west Ireland and the Irish Sea spawn, is over the deep water of about 180 m (100 fathoms) near the edge of the continental shelf, about 100 miles west of the Scilly Isles.

Spawning starts furthest out to the west in March, and moves slowly eastwards, reaching its height in April and extending into June. During this time, huge shoals of mackerel feed on plank-tonic copepods and krill. These shoals are fished for with drift-nets, and in 1972 10,300 tons, worth £480,000, were landed, but this represents the total landings all round Britain. The main fishery ends when the shoals break up and move inshore. It is during the inshore period that mackerel are caught by anglers and holidaymakers.

The spawning season is long, not only because different fish ripen at different times, but also because the eggs in each individual ripen in batches over a period. The eggs and fry float a little below the surface. Growth is rapid; after one year the mackerel average about 24 cm (9½ in.), at two about 31 cm (12¼ in.) and at five years of age about 36 cm (14 in.). They mature when two years old.

The other common member of this family is the **tunny**, *Thunnus thynnus* (Plate 34), which in America is called the tuna. Since most canned tunny comes from America, we tend to associate tuna only with canned fish.

The tunny grows into a huge fish of over 360 cm (12 ft) and 680 kg (1500 lb), but the British rod-caught record is at 385·989 kg (851 lb) for one caught off Whitby in 1933. The body is thickset, with two dorsal fins close together. The pectoral, pelvic, second dorsal and tail fins are very narrow and scythe-shaped. The first dorsal fin lies flat in a groove and the paired fins fit into depressions on the side of the body, so that the surface is quite smooth with no interruptions to the flow of the water round the body. It is indeed a remarkably streamlined fish, and it inhabits the mid and surface waters where it feeds on herring, pilchards, mackerel, sandeels, and flying fish, as well as squid.

The back of the tunny is dark blue and the sides are lighter, while the belly is silvery white.

The second dorsal and anal fins are reddish brown, and the others are dark blue.

The usual home of the tunny is the warmer waters of the Mediterranean and off Spain, Portugal and North Africa. However, they make regular migrations northwards and into the North Sea, where a sport fishery has developed at Scarborough and Whitby on the Yorkshire coast. Here they appear in mid-July and depart again in October. Two large tunny which were marked with numbered tags off the Bahamas were caught off Bergen less than four months later. This, and other evidence, suggests that transatlantic migrations may be common, and probably in summer tunny range over very large areas of the North Atlantic.

The flesh of fresh tunny is red and very nutritious. It forms the basis of an important canning industry in America and the canned meat, which also has an excellent flavour, is rather oily and brown.

Another migrant from warmer waters is the **bonito**, *Sarda sarda*. This is a small tunny which rarely exceeds 70 cm (27½ in.) and is distinguishable by having dark blue stripes running diagonally up the body.

Other species which occasionally stray as far as Britain are the **oceanic bonito**, *Katsuwonus pelamis*, which is never common, and the **frigate mackerel**, *Auxis thazard*, the **long-finned tunny**, *Thunnus alalunga*, and the **Spanish mackerel**, *Scomber colias*, all of which are rare.

The Swordfishes XIPHIIDAE

The **swordfish**, *Xiphias gladius*, is a remarkable creature with a long sword on the head like a fishy unicorn. But it is a real fish which is commonest in tropical and subtropical waters, and is only infrequently reported round Britain. The sword makes it recognizable immediately. It grows to a large size, even up to nearly 5 m (16 ft). It is said that the sword is used to disable small fish as it charges through their shoals, striking to left and right. Then the swordfish is said to come back to eat its victims. Certainly it is hard to see how the swordfish could eat fish by skewering them with its sword. Probably most of the incidents of boats and whales having been speared are due to some accident or misjudgement on the fish's part.

The Gobies GOBIIDAE

The gobies are some of the most abundant shore fishes and also the most difficult for the layman to identify. Even the professional marine biologist has to seek the help of the expert with some species. It is easy to know if a fish is a goby; the difficulty is in telling which goby.

The most conspicuous characteristic of the family is that the pelvic fins have become modified to form a sucker. This has happened in three other groups of fishes, the lumpsuckers, the sea snails and the cling fish. If the fish with a pectoral fin sucker has conspicuous scales and two dorsal fins, it is a goby (Plates 37, 40, 44). If it has horny tubercles, it is a lumpsucker (Plate 53). If it has no scales or tubercles and has a single long dorsal fin and a long anal fin, the fish is a sea snail (Page 39). If the dorsal and anal fins are both short and near the tail, the specimen is a clingfish (Plate 43). The different shapes of the suckers are shown below.

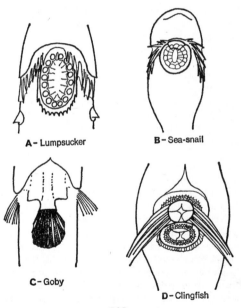

A - Lumpsucker

B - Sea-snail

C - Goby

D - Clingfish

All the gobies are small and most are bottom-living fish in shallow water or near the beach. They have large heads and tapering bodies. They tend to be rather squat, and their bulging eyes are set near the top of the head. Both of these characteristics are associated with their bottom-living habit. They have two dorsal fins.

The males, which in many species are differently coloured from the females, defend a nest site which is usually under stones or inside bivalve shells. After the eggs have been laid and fertilized the males continue to guard them. These eggs are vase-shaped and attached by the base, and are laid in groups.

There are two gobies which have taken to a life off the bottom. The **crystal goby**, *Crystallogobius linearis*, which has at most only two rays in the first dorsal fin, and the **transparent goby**, *Aphia minuta*, with five rays, are both probably commoner than is supposed. Not only are they remarkably transparent, but also they are very easily damaged when caught in a net. Furthermore, because of their small size (up to 4 cm: $1\frac{1}{2}$ in.) and surface and mid-water swimming habits, they are rarely caught.

The **two-spot goby**, *Chaparrudo flavescens*, is perhaps intermediate between the two pelagic species described above and the typical gobies considered next. Although living inshore, it is not obviously dependent on the bottom and is most often seen swimming in shoals around seaweed. In the two-spot goby, and the two pelagic species, the eyes are not near the top of the head, but on the sides, which is a more advantageous place for their way of life in mid- or surface waters.

The two-spot goby, which rarely grows above 6 cm (2½ in.), can be identified by its two black spots, one at the base of the tail, and the other under the pectoral fin. (There are of course two spots on each side, making four in all.) The body is a rufous brown with four light patches on the dorsal surface. This fish is common round most of Britain.

Of the typical gobies, the **common goby**, *Pomatoschistus microps*, is probably the most abundant and widespread. It is found on sandy and muddy shores, in estuaries and similar places where fresh water reduces the salinity. It is even found in fresh water. In these localities it occurs in intertidal pools and drains, even if there are only a few centimetres or so of water. The caudal peduncle (between the dorsal fin and the tail) is long, and the colour is greyish with clusters of small spots forming a row down each side. The dorsal fins have dark bars over both the membranes and rays.

Another abundant goby, but this time one less tolerant of reduced salinity, and less often found intertidally, is the **sand goby**, *Pomatoschistus minutus*. This species also has a long caudal peduncle, but the body is a light brown rather than grey, and there is a conspicuous black spot at the back of the first dorsal fin. The sand goby grows to 10 cm (4 in.) and is found all round the British Isles. It likes depths of 30 cm to 36 m (12 in. to 20 fathoms) and is very often caught by shrimpers fishing over sandy ground.

During the spawning season, from April to the end of August, the pear-shaped eggs are laid in empty bivalve shells and then guarded by the male. Most adults die after spawning, during their second summer. The young are planktonic until about 12 mm long, when they take to the bottom.

The **painted goby**, *Pomatoschistus pictus* (Plate 40), like *P. microps* and *P. minutus*, has a long caudal peduncle and is also characterized by rows of black spots between each ray on the two dorsal fins, which also often bear bands of red. The colour of the back is a medium brown, and each scale edge is picked out in a darker colour which gives a network pattern. There are four lighter areas across the back. This fish grows to 6 cm (2·4 in.).

The painted goby lives from low tide mark to about 27 m (15 fathoms) on sandy and rocky ground all round the British Isles. The breeding season is in spring and summer when the pear-shaped eggs are laid in empty sea-shells and are guarded by the male.

The **black goby**, *Gobius niger* (Plate 44), is one of the gobies with a short caudal peduncle. The two dorsal fins are joined by a membrane at the base. The scales are large and conspicuous. The black goby is a dark grey or brown rather than black, and has irregular lighter patterns.

This species is mainly estuarine, but it also occurs where the water is fully saline in sandy and muddy bays. It is found all round Britain. Like other gobies, it mainly eats crustacea belonging to the isopod, amphipod and mysid groups, as well as small crabs, shrimps and other crustacea, some worms and small molluscs.

The **rock goby**, *Gobius paganellus* (Plate 37), also has a relatively small length of body between the dorsal fin and the tail (the caudal peduncle). It has a large head with its eyes on the top. The body varies from black to reddish brown, and the dorsal fins have conspicuous white or yellow margins. This fish grows to 12 cm (4¾ in.).

The rock goby is found from mid-tide level to below low tide mark on rocky coasts. It is found in rock pools and under stones. It is absent from the North Sea coasts and the north of Scotland, but is very common round the rest of Britain.

There are numerous other rare gobies, of which we can mention only a few here. The **giant goby**, *Gobius cobitis*, grows to 25 cm (10 in.) and is the largest species. It is found only on the Channel coasts off Cornwall, Devon and Dorset, where it inhabits rock pools. It is dark grey with light brown flecks and black spots. The belly is lighter.

Fries' goby, *Lesueurigobius friesii* (Plate 37), is an offshore, deep-water species that is found in the Irish Sea and off the west coasts of Ireland and Scotland. In the Clyde area it is common in the deep water on a muddy bottom. It can be recognized by the rows of conspicuous papillae on the sides of the head, and by the yellow markings on a light grey or brown background.

Another deep-water species is **Jeffrey's goby**, *Buenia jeffreysii*, which can be distinguished by its characteristic coloration of pale grey mottled with orange and brown. There are five black spots on each side of the body, and smaller spots on the dorsal fins. Jeffrey's goby is found on muddy sand and shell gravel, and probably is not as rare as its patchy distribution record suggests. It grows to over 5 cm (2 in.).

A small 3 to 4 cm (about 1½ in.) goby is the **diminutive goby**, *Lebetus orca* (Plate 40). It does not appear to have a wide distribution or to be very common, but this may be because of its small size and its offshore habitat of coarse shell gravel, stones and sand. It can be recognized by the almost colourless area between the dorsal fin and the tail. The body is yellowish brown with four dark bands.

Work on the natural history of British gobies is being done by a few dedicated zoologists, and new species have been found and the range of rare species extended. One recent addition is the **leopard-spotted goby**, *Thorogobius ephippiatus* (= *Gobius forsteri*) which, because of its habit of hiding in crevices in very rocky ground, was only discovered when scientists began skin-diving. Another species, *G. cruentatus*, has been found wrongly identified in three museum collections made in south-west Ireland. It is mainly a Mediterranean species that extends to the Atlantic coasts of Spain, southern France and now apparently to Ireland.

The Dragonets CALLIONYMIDAE

The dragonets are such extraordinary-looking fish that after one glance at Plates 41 and 48 they are unlikely to be confused with any other species. From their slightly flattened shape they are obviously bottom-living fish, and they often lie half buried in sand or gravel. They are mainly found in fairly shallow inshore water. The males have very bright and striking colour patterns, but the females are remarkably drab. There are three British species.

The **common dragonet**, *Callionymus lyra* (Plate 48), is the most abundant species and is found all round the British Isles. The mature males have extremely long dorsal fin rays, and the yellow second dorsal fin has bright iridescent blue lengthwise stripes. The females are a drab variegated light and dark brown, and the second dorsal fin has rather faint darker longitudinal stripes.

The striking sexual colour differences are associated with the remarkable courtship display put on by the male. After driving away rival males from his prospective mate, the male dragonet puffs out his mouth and gill-covers, so making his head appear twice the normal size.

At the same time he swims in front of the female with fins raised, which displays the gorgeous iridescent blue stripes. In the actual pairing, the two fish leave the bottom and swim together towards the surface, with the female resting on the male's pectoral fin in such a way that the eggs from the female and the milt from the male are shed together into the water.

The male may be up to 30 cm (12 in.) in length and the female up to 20 cm (8 in.). In 1973 a record dragonet of 128 g (4½ oz) was caught off Bexhill.

The **spotted dragonet**, *Callionymus maculatus* (Plate 41), is smaller than the previous species and can be distinguished by having lengthwise rows of dark spots along the second dorsal fin where the common dragonet had stripes. These spots need not be confused with the spots on the fin of the third species, *C. reticulatus*. Here the spots are situated in bluish wavy bands which are predominantly vertical and have dark margins.

The spotted dragonet grows to 14 cm (5½ in.) though the females are smaller (11 cm or 4½ in.). The sides have conspicuous brown and blue spots as well as variegated brown markings. The spotted dragonet is found mostly on the west coasts from the western Channel to the Orkney Isles, mainly in deepish water and on offshore banks.

Callionymus reticulatus is found in shallower water, and since its discovery in 1951 in the western Channel, has been recorded only from the

Irish Sea, the southern North Sea and County Galway.

The Blennies   BLENNIIDAE

The blennies are small inshore fish of no economic importance. However, they are the commonest fish on rocky shores and in rock pools, and they are widely distributed.

Most blennies have a large head and tapering body. The skin is without scales. They have a single dorsal fin which in some species is divided into two sections by a notch. In a few species the dorsal fin is continuous with the tail and anal fins.

The form of the dorsal fin can be used to divide the blennies into three groups. In the first, the Blenniidae proper, the dorsal fin has the typical blenny notch, and it is not joined to the tail fin. The commonest species in this group is the **shanny**, *Blennius pholis* (Plate 35), which grows to 15 cm (6 in.). The dip in the dorsal fin is only very slight, and the shanny is the only member of this group without tentacles on the head. The shanny is a dark greenish brown with variegated light and dark brown blotches.

The shanny is found all round Britain on all kinds of coasts, but it prefers shallow rocky areas with boulders, ledges, pools and crevices. Spawning takes place in summer and the eggs, which are laid in a crevice or under a stone, are guarded by the male. As well as chasing off intruders, he fans water over the clumps of eggs with his fins for six to eight weeks, until the young hatch out.

The shanny eats crustacea such as isopods, amphipods, crabs and barnacles, as well as a wide variety of molluscs and other animals and algae.

All the other species of blennies in this group have one or more crests on top of the head. In the case of the **tompot blenny**, *Blennius gattorugine*, there are two branched tentacles, one above each eye. The first portion of the dorsal fin is slightly lower than the second, and the rays are stiffer. It is yellowish or greenish brown with dark vertical bars that are more pronounced towards the tail. It grows to 30 cm (12 in.) and is the largest blenny.

The tompot blenny is more often caught offshore than are the other blennies, and it is taken in trawls and in crabpots. It is mainly recorded from the south and west coasts, though even here it is not common.

Another blenny found in the 10 to 20 m range (5½–11 fathoms) is the **butterfly blenny** *Blennius ocellaris* (Plate 38). In this species also there is a branched tentacle over each eye, but the rays in the first section of the dorsal fin are over twice as long as those of the second, and there is a very conspicuous black spot, ringed with white, on the membrane of the first part of the dorsal fin.

The butterfly blenny grows to 18 cm (7 in.)

and is found only on the south-west coasts of
England and Ireland, and in the Irish Sea.

Montagu's blenny, *Coryphoblennius galerita*
(Plate 35), may be recognized by the fold of skin
which forms a fringed crest running across the
head between the eyes. The whole of the body,
and all the fins, except the anal, have bluish-
white spots on a greenish-brown background.
It is a small blenny and rarely exceeds 8 cm
(3 in.).

Montagu's blenny has a restricted habitat and
range. It is found only between tide marks,
most often on the upper half of the shore, and
only on south-western coasts of England, Wales
and Ireland.

The Butterfish   PHOLIDIDAE

This family, together with the Lumpenidae and
Stichaeidae, form the second group of blenny-
like fishes. In this group the long dorsal fin is
the same height all the way along and does not
have the typical blenny notch. The dorsal and
anal fins come very close to the caudal fin, but
do not actually join it.

The best-known member of this group is the
butterfish, *Pholis gunnellus* (Plate 45). It is
extremely plentiful and is found all round the
British Isles. It occurs on the shore and also
below low tide mark. Besides the arrangement
of the fin, the butterfish has very distinctive
colouring. It is golden or mustard-brown and

has a row of black spots, each of which has a white halo, along the base of the dorsal fin. The head is small and the pelvic fins are minute. The long body is laterally flattened, and the butterfish is one of the slipperiest fishes on British shores. Its food consists of all kinds of small crustacea and worms.

Yarrell's Blenny STICHAEIDAE

Yarrell's blenny, *Chirolophis ascanii* (Plate 35), also has a long even dorsal fin which is not connected with the tail. However, whereas the butterfish does not have any crests, Yarrell's blenny has a fringed tentacle above each eye, as well as small ones behind each nostril. The dorsal fin has rather stiff spiny rays. The body, which is a yellowish brown with darker bands, has minute scales.

Yarrell's blenny has a patchy distribution and is nowhere common. It is found off the coasts of Devon, Cornwall, Yorkshire, western Scotland and in the Irish Sea.

Snake Blenny LUMPENIDAE

The **snake blenny**, *Lumpenus lumpretaeformis*, is a relatively deep-water species which is found around Greenland, Iceland, Norway and Scotland, where it is commonest on a muddy bottom. It can be recognized by its very long pale brown body with darker brown blotches. The tail fin,

which is separate from the dorsal and anal fins,
is long.

Viviparous Blenny ZOARCIDAE

The **viviparous blenny**, *Zoarces viviparus*
(Plate 38), belongs to the third blenny group in
which the dorsal, caudal and anal fins are continuous. Very near the end of the dorsal fin
there is a slight dip where the spines are weaker.
The body is long and eel-like, and tapers gradu-
ally from the head to the pointed tail. The body
is a yellowish brown with faint darker markings
and round lighter blotches on the sides. It
grows to 46 cm (18 in.). The British rod-caught
record is for a viviparous blenny of 326 g
(11½ oz) caught near Rhu in the Clyde, in
1972. This blenny is found mostly on the
eastern side of England and round the Scottish
coasts.

The viviparous blenny is peculiar in that it
does not lay eggs, but brings forth live young
that are small replicas of the parents. The male
has a small elongated papilla by means of which
the milt is introduced into the female, and the
eggs are fertilized in the ovary. Whereas most
fish have paired ovaries, in the viviparous blenny
there is only a single ovary. The young hatch
from the eggs about three weeks after fertilization, but remain in the body of the female for
another three months. At first they live on the
yolk of the egg, but later receive nourishment

from a fluid secreted by the walls of the ovary. When they emerge from the mother they are 4 cm (1½ in.) long. A small female will bear about forty young, but larger parents give birth to over three hundred.

The Catfishes ANARHICHADIDAE

The catfishes are deep-water northern cousins of the blennies, and they grow to a much larger size. Two species are landed at British fishing ports, but only one is found locally. Both have large pointed canine teeth in the front of the jaw and flat crushing molars behind. They differ from blennies in having no pelvic fins (in the true blennies these fins are always present, though sometimes minute). The dorsal fin is long and not joined to the caudal.

The **catfish**, *Anarhichas lupus* (Plate 44), grows to 150 cm (60 in.) and its colour is very reminiscent of a tabby cat. The background is a dark blue or greenish grey with black transverse stripes over the body and fins. The head is blunt, and the jaws are very powerful and can deal with the hard shelled food which consists of whelks, clams, crabs, hermit crabs, sea-urchins and other bottom creatures. The catfish is found mainly offshore in deep water round the northern half of Britain. It is landed in considerable quantities. In 1972 5900 tons, worth £500,000, were landed at British ports. However, it is such a fearsome and ugly-looking creature that it is first decapi-

tated and skinned, and then sold as 'rock salmon'
or 'rockfish'.   These names are given to a variety
of species including the dogfish, the monkfish,
Squatina squatina, and the angler, *Lophius piscatorius*, all of which, while perfectly wholesome,
would not appeal to the housewife in their
natural state.   The catfish is sometimes caught
by anglers and the British rod-caught record is
for a catfish of 4·422 kg (9¾ lb) caught at Stone-
haven in 1971.

Like the blennies, the catfish lays sticky eggs
in large clumps on the sea floor.   At first the
young live near the bottom and, later, in mid-
water before they return to the bottom as
juveniles.

The second species, the **spotted catfish**,
Anarhichas minor, grows to over 1·82 m (6 ft).
It can be distinguished by its dark brown spots
rather than stripes.   It has a more northerly
distribution than *A. lupus*.

The Black-fish   CENTROLOPHIDAE

The **black-fish**, *Centrolophus niger*, is a rare
oceanic fish, found from Spain to Iceland and
Norway at depths of about 550 m (300 fathoms).
It is a longish fish with a rounded head and single
dorsal and anal fins.   The tail fin is well forked.
The fins and the back are a dull black and the
belly is silvery.   It grows to 85 cm (33 in.).   In
1967 one was caught in Lough Foyle, Northern

Ireland, another off County Cork, and a third near the Shetland Isles. Seven were caught in 1968, one of which was from the North Sea. The record rod-caught specimen was 1·658 kg (3 lb 10½ oz) from off the Heads of Ayr in 1972.

The Grey Mullets MUGILIDAE

The grey mullets are not related to the red mullet, and it is unfortunate that they should have such similar names. Until recently there has been considerable confusion over the number of species and their natural history, but during the last decade some work has been done on these species and has removed much of the confusion.

The **grey mullets** (Plate 47) are mostly southern species which migrate into British coastal waters during the summer. They are thick and well streamlined, with large scales and two well-spaced dorsal fins. The back is a leaden blue-grey and the underparts are paler.

The **thick-lipped mullet**, *Crenimugil labrosus*, can be identified by the thickness of the upper lip, which is equal to about half the diameter of the eye. In the two other species the upper lip is considerably thinner and is much less than half the eye diameter. These two species with thin lips can be separated by the length of the pectoral fin. In the **golden mullet**, *Liza auratus*, the fin almost reaches to vertically below the beginning of the first dorsal fin. In the **thin-lipped mullet**, *Liza ramada*, the pectoral fin barely reaches half the distance. The golden mullet has golden spots on the head and a golden tint on the flanks, and these characteristics are missing from the thin-lipped species.

All three grey mullets are essentially marine fish and they migrate inshore in summer. They are often seen swimming lazily on the surface in huge shoals. The thick-lipped and thin-lipped mullets come into harbours and estuaries, and even into freshwater rivers. The golden mullet, however, is never found in fresh water.

The three mullets feed in much the same way. They do not have any teeth in the mouth and the pharyngeal teeth are modified to form part of a filtering apparatus. They feed by sucking up a mixture of soil and small particles of plants and animals. The large particles of soil are spat out and the finer particles act as a grinding paste. Besides detritus in the soil, the fish consume small algae and animals such as harpacticoids, copepods and nematodes. They also scrape off the felt of microscopic plants that grow on rocks, piers and seaweeds. The contents of many stomachs that have been examined have been found to contain over 85% indigestible matter. In developing these peculiar feeding habits the grey mullets exploit a source of food which is not eaten by any other kind of fish. In order to extract the maximum value from the food, they have developed a grinding 'gizzard' at the hind end of the stomach, and the intestines are up to five times the length of the fish. This is a greater gut length than is found in other fish, and allows greater absorption of food material. The thick-lipped mullet reaches 9 cm (3½ in.) at two years of age, 30 cm (12 in.) at six, 42 cm (16½ in.) at nine, and 50 cm (20 in.) at twelve years old. The thin-lipped species grows faster and reaches 12 cm (4¾ in.) at two and 33 cm (13 in.) at six years of age. The golden mullet grows to 11 cm (4½ in.) at two, and 30 to 34 cm (12–13 in.) at six years of age.

The thick-lipped mullet spawns in April and May in the sea, but although one spawning place is near the Scilly Isles, very little else is known. The thin-lipped mullet is also thought to spawn at sea, but probably in the autumn. Nothing is known about the breeding of the golden mullet.

Because of their specialized feeding habits, grey mullets are rarely caught by anglers. However, there is a British rod-caught record of 4·564 kg (10 lb 1 oz) for a thick-lipped mullet caught off Portland in 1952, and of 0·805 kg (1 lb 12 oz 7 dm) for a golden mullet from Alderney in 1973, and 1·360 kg (3 lb) for a thin-lipped mullet in 1973 from Kent. Not only are these mullets difficult to catch on a hook and line, but they are also difficult to surround with a net. When they appear to be nicely caught by a seine net being dragged up on to the shore, the whole shoal will escape by jumping over the top of the net. The total British landings in 1970 only amounted to 50 tons, worth £10,000.

The Sand Smelts ATHERINIDAE

The sand smelts must not be confused with the true smelt, which is a member of the Osmeridae and is related to the salmon family and has a small adipose fin. The sand smelt has a short bluntish head and two well-spaced dorsal fins. The colour is also distinctive. The upper parts are green and the belly is silver. Each scale is picked out by small black dots, and down each side is a brilliant silver band.

The **sand smelt**, *Atherina presbyter* (Plate 39), migrates in large shoals into inshore and coastal water during the summer. It is particularly common in estuarine and other waters of low salinity. From 1955 to 1963 another species, **Boyer's sand smelt**, *A. mochon*, was found in two warm docks, one in Swansea and the other in Barrow-in-Furness. It can be distinguished by its larger head and relatively smaller scales.

The sand smelt spawns in June and July, and the eggs stick in long strings to seaweed and any other solid object on the sea floor. Often the shoals are seen in large shore pools, and the eggs may be laid there. The sand smelt grows to 15 cm (6 in.) and although it is very good to eat, a lot is needed to make a worthwhile meal. They can be cooked like sprats, and the fry are sometimes cooked along with other fish as whitebait. One of 31 g (1 oz 2 dm), caught off Jersey in 1973, is the British rod-caught record.

The Red-Fish   SCORPAENIDAE

The only common species in this family are the red-fish or Norway haddock and the blue-mouth. There are two species of **red-fish** and they are very similar. In *Sebastes viviparus* (Plate 45), the spines on the pre-opercular bone (the flat bone in front of the gill-cover bone) all point backwards, while in *S. marinus* the lower three spines point downwards. The dorsal fin of both species is long and is in two portions, the first with strong spines and the posterior part with soft branched rays. The head is large, spiny and with large eyes. Both species are bright vermilion with some darker markings on the gill-covers and sides. *S. viviparus* is the smaller, more coastal species and not of great economic importance. It is sometimes caught by anglers, and the British rod-caught record is at 538 g (1 lb 3 oz) for one caught off Southend Pier in 1973. *S. marinus* on the other hand grows to 1 m (3 ft) in length and is of very considerable importance commercially. It is a deep-water fish which rarely comes close to Britain but is caught in very large numbers by trawlers and landed at British ports. In 1972 the landings totalled 9150 tons, worth £502,000.

Both species of red-fish are ovoviviparous.

In the Barents Sea mating takes place in August and September, and in November and December the fish migrate south. Fertilization of the eggs is delayed until February or March and the young are born in May and June. The young are born as larvae, that is, they have used up all the yolk reserves in growth, but have not yet assumed the fin characters and other features of the adult form.

The **blue-mouth**, *Helicolenus dactylopterus*, is a rare fish living on the edge of the continental shelf in 150–800 m (80–440 fathoms); it is occasionally reported inshore. The inside of the mouth is blue and the body is red above and pink below. The head is very spiny and has large eyes. One blue-mouth of 1·198 kg (2 lb 10¼ oz) was caught in Loch Shell, The Minch, in 1974 and it holds the British rod-caught record.

The Gurnards TRIGLIDAE

The gurnards are bottom-living fish with a very peculiar and angular appearance. The head region is strongly armoured with bony plates. These plates, as well as the operculum and pre-operculum, have strong spines which make the gurnards awkward fish to handle. The skin is tough and in many species there are spines along the lateral line. The head is large and the body tapers evenly from the region of the gills to the tail. The most characteristic feature of the gurnards, however, is the modification of the pectoral fin. The lower three rays are free from the rest of the fin and do not have any membrane connecting them. These rays have become feeling organs with which the gurnards search the sea floor for food. Gurnards also make grunting noises by contracting muscles round the swim-bladder. These sounds are said to keep the fish together as they wander in loosely knit shoals over the bottom.

Some gurnards are landed by fishing boats, and in 1972 they amounted to 700 tons, valued at £41,000.

The commonest species in this family is the **grey gurnard**, *Eutrigla gurnardus* (Plate 49). It can be recognized by its grey or dark brown colour and sharply pointed scales along the lateral line. There are small white spots scattered over the body. The pectoral fin is short and does not reach the anal fin.

The food of the grey gurnard consists mainly of crustacea, such as shrimps, prawns and small crabs. It apparently finds these with the aid of its pectoral fin feelers.

The grey gurnard is found all round the British Isles, particularly on sandy or gravelly ground. It is the commonest gurnard and although sometimes found close to the shore, is mainly in 20–40 m (10–20 fathoms). Spawning takes place in the spring, and the eggs and larvae are pelagic. This species grows to 40 cm (16 in.).

The British rod-caught record is 963 g (2 lb 2 oz) for a grey gurnard caught at Port Rush, N.Ireland.

Another species which is sometimes found close inshore is the **tub gurnard**, *Trigla lucerna* (Plate 42). It has a number of other common names, such as the yellow or saphirine gurnard. It can be identified easily by the colour of the pectoral fins, which are deep blue on the inner surface and an orange-red with blue bands and green spots round the edge. These fins are long and reach beyond the start of the anal fin. The scales along the lateral line are smooth. The tub gurnard is a large species. The British rod-caught record specimen was 5·195 kg (11 lb 7¼ oz) and was caught at Wallasey in 1952.

The tub gurnard is a southern species which lives mainly on sandy or gravelly ground from western Ireland to the southern North Sea. It is rare north of East Anglia, and on the west coast is rarer in the Irish Sea and round the coasts of Scotland.

The young specimens eat crustacea, but the larger ones eat fish such as dragonets and solenettes.

The **red gurnard**, *Aspitrigla cuculus* (Plate 42), is the smallest of the three common gurnards. It grows to 30 cm (12 in.) and the British rod-caught record is 2·268 kg (5 lb) for one caught off Rhyl in 1973. It is commonest on the west coast, where it extends to the north of Scotland, whereas on the east coast it is only common in the southern North Sea. The scales along the lateral line are in the form of narrow plates without spines. The red gurnard spawns around midsummer. Like other gurnards, it feeds mainly on shrimps, prawns, small crabs and small fish.

The sides of the **streaked gurnard**, *Triglo-porus lastoviza* (Plate 49), are covered with ridges across the body, which is a deep red. The long orange-red pectoral fins have bands of blue spots. There are also blue lines on the first dorsal fin. The head is blunt, with a shorter snout than that of other gurnards. It is an uncommon southern and western species. It grows to 35 cm (14 in.). The rod-caught record for this species is 637 g (1 lb 6½ oz) for one in 1971 from L. Goil.

There are two other southern gurnards, the **piper**, *Trigla lyra*, and the **long-finned gurnard** *Aspitrigla obscura*, which are very occasionally reported from south-west England, and are too rare to warrant description here.

The Sea-scorpions COTTIDAE

Although the species in this family are sometimes called bullheads, the American name sculpin is becoming used more often.

The sea-scorpion is a ferocious-looking fish with a large head, which is slightly flattened, and a huge mouth. There is always an array of very sharp spines, particularly on the gill-covers. There are no scales on the body.

There are two common marine species, the largest of which is the **short-spined sea-scorpion**, *Myoxocephalus scorpius*, also known as the bull rout or father lasher. It grows to 30 cm (12 in.), but is rare over 23 cm (9 in.). The British rod-caught record is for one of 977 g (2 lb 2½ oz) caught in 1972 at Sunderland. It has only two prominent opercular spines. On the underside, by the throat, there is a membrane stretching across from the gill-covers on each side, which forms a sort of pocket in the mid line. This membrane is lacking in the next species and so is a very important point in identification.

The body tapers rapidly from the very broad head to the tail. The upper parts are a mottled and variegated brown. The belly is paler and the sides have round light spots. Occasionally the belly is yellow or orange, particularly in ripe females.

This sea-scorpion is found in deeper water than the next species, although specimens may be found intertidally in the north. It is predominantly a fish of rocky ground though it also occurs on sand and rarely on mud. It is distributed all round the British Isles.

Spawning takes place in the winter and early spring and is probably similar to that described under the long-spined species, though hatching is earlier and so is the planktonic larval stage which ends in April or May.

The **long-spined sea scorpion**, *Taurulus bubalis* (Plate 52), is smaller than the previous species, which it resembles closely. The membrane from the gill-covers on the underside does not join right across to form a flap, and the uppermost spine on the gill-covers is very long. The coloration is similar to the short-spined species. This fish grows to 20 cm (8 in.). The British rod-caught record of 66 g (2 oz 5 dm) was caught off Guernsey in 1974.

The long-spined sea-scorpion is a more littoral species than the previous one. It is often found between tide marks on rocky ground among seaweed. It eats a wide variety of crustacea, worms and small fish.

This species spawns in early spring. There is a fairly elaborate courtship in which the male turns and darts rapidly in front of the female, stopping repeatedly to display his coloured fins which are erected and twitched in front of her. The eggs are laid in a natural crevice or a hollow made by the male. The orange-coloured eggs are laid in masses and contain a lot of yolk material which is used up during their development. The male guards the eggs until they hatch. The larvae, which are quite large, are planktonic throughout the early summer.

The long-spined sea-scorpion is found all round the British Isles.

A much rarer deep-water species is the **Norway bullhead**, *Taurulus lilljeborgi*. As in *T. bubalis*, the gill-cover membrane does not form a flap, but it is distinguished by its rough skin with small spines on the back. It grows to

6 cm (2½ in.) and has been found in the Firth of
Forth and several isolated places on the Scottish
and Irish west coasts, and Isle of Man.

Triglops murrayi, which has ridges on the lower
half of the body, is a very rare northern species
recorded from off Kintyre, Northern Ireland, and
the Shetland Isles.

The Pogge   AGONIDAE

The **pogge** or **armed bullhead**, *Agonus cataphractus* (Plate 29), is one of our more bizarre
sea fishes. It has a large head and a long thin
tail. There are two dorsal fins and one anal.
The body, which is brown with darker patches,
is covered with hard plates. There are sharp
spines on the gill-covers and on the long snout.
The underside of the head, which is a creamy
white, is covered with a mass of small barbels.
The pogge grows to 15 cm (6 in.).

The pogge spawns during the early winter,
and the eggs, which are laid in clumps, take three
months to hatch. The young, after a planktonic
stage, take to the bottom during the summer.
The pogge is a bottom-living fish and is very
common all round Britain, particularly on hard
ground.

The Lumpsucker   CYCLOPTERIDAE

The **lumpsucker**, *Cyclopterus lumpus* (Plate 53),
is a very odd-looking fish and is unlikely to be

confused with any other. Although not spherical, it has a very globular shape. The head and body are covered with some bony tubercles arranged quite haphazardly, and others in seven definite rows. One row is down the mid line of the back, and there are three rows on each side, which run from the head to the tail. These tubercles are sharply pointed. Another very conspicuous feature is the sucker formed from the pelvic fins. On page 121 we have already described the other families of fish that have suckers formed from the pelvic fins and how these families may be distinguished. The suckers are illustrated on that page.

The colour of the lumpsucker is usually grey and lighter on the underside. During the breeding season they take on an orange or reddish tint. The adult fish has one anal and one dorsal fin, but the juveniles have two dorsal fins. The first one, which is rather fleshy, disappears as the lumpsucker becomes adult.

The female lumpsucker grows to 60 cm (24 in.) but the male rarely exceeds 50 cm (20 in.). The British rod-caught record is 6·435 kg (14 lb 3 oz) for one caught off Felixstowe in 1970. They are found all round the British Isles both offshore and sometimes between tide marks.

The male lumpsucker is renowned for his solicitude for the eggs. Breeding usually takes place below low tide mark during March and April. After the eggs are laid the female returns to deep water, but the male stays with them, attached to the rock by his sucker, and for six or seven weeks he fans a current of well-aerated water over them. In Scotland, and on northern shores, they sometimes breed inter-tidally and the male remains with the eggs even when the tide has gone down. At this time they are very vulnerable to birds, rats and other predators.

The Sea Snails LIPARIDAE

These small fish are superficially more reminiscent of a tadpole than a snail. The head is blunt and the body tapers to the tail from the widest part just behind the gill-covers. The most conspicuous characteristic is a very powerful sucker which is a modification of the pelvic fins. Families of fishes with this kind of modified fin were described and illustrated on page 121. The development of a sucker has gone farther in the sea snails than in the other families, and it is a very powerful circular disc hardly recognizable as the fin from which it has evolved.

There are two British species in this family. The **sea snail**, *Liparis liparis*, is the larger, and usually lives offshore. It grows to 18 cm (7 in.) and is a northern species which is found north-wards from Wales and from the Thames estuary.

Montagu's sea snail, *Liparis montagui* (Plate 39), rarely exceeds 6 cm (2½ in.) and is an inshore and littoral species. It is found around most of the British Isles apart from the south-east. The two species are very similar. In *L. liparis* the anal fin is joined to the caudal fin by a membrane, whereas in Montagu's sea snail the two fins are not actually joined, though the anal fin membrane may reach the base of the caudal fin. The fins are yellowish. Both species are usually a dull grey and have very variable markings which cannot be used for identification.

The Sticklebacks GASTEROSTEIDAE

The sticklebacks are small fish of under 20 cm (8 in.). They have two dorsal fins but the first has no membrane between the rays which are in the form of sharp spines. The number of these spines is the chief characteristic used in identifying sticklebacks.

The **ten-spined stickleback**, *Pungitius pungitius*, is really a freshwater fish, but occasionally it lives in brackish water. It is found on the eastern sides of England and Ireland, and in southern Scotland. The **three-spined stickleback**, *Gasterosteus aculeatus*, is another freshwater fish, but it is often found in shore pools and even several miles out in the open sea.

The three-spined stickleback is very common in such places as seaside boating ponds, and high-level pools which are flushed out at high tide and also have fresh water draining in. There are three dorsal spines, but the third is very small and close to the dorsal fin. The pelvic fin is composed of a single spine. The marine specimens are silvery blue above, and have a row of well-developed bony plates from the head to tail along the lateral line. This stickleback grows to between 6 and 10 cm (2½–4 in.).

The male builds a nest from plant material stuck together with a special kidney secretion. He induces a female to lay her eggs in this nest and, after he has fertilized them, he guards and aerates them until they hatch in about two weeks. In the sea this stickleback mainly eats small crustacea.

The **fifteen-spined stickleback**, *Spinachia spinachia* (Plate 41), is the largest species and grows to 20 cm (8 in.). It is abundant on rocky coasts and shore pools all round Britain. It is a long, thin fish with a long head, and its tail is on the end of a long caudal peduncle. There are fourteen to sixteen spines immediately followed by the dorsal fin, below which is the anal fin. The pelvic fin consists of a single spine. The fifteen-spined stickleback is brown above and silvery below. Breeding males have a bluish colour and the females are greenish. The male makes a nest about 8 cm (3 in.) in diameter among seaweed and it is composed of plant material bound together by a kidney secretion. The female spawns in the nest some time in May or June. The male guards the eggs for about three weeks. The food of the fifteen-spined stickleback consists of plankton and also small shore and bottom-living crustacea.

The Flatfishes

There are three families in the Order Hetero-
somata, but as they share some features and differ
in others, it is worth while to consider all the
flatfishes together before we look at the different
families.

The flatfish are bottom-living fishes, but whereas the rays and skates swim on their stomachs,
the flatfish swim on their sides. There are
various problems for a fish that lives on the sea
floor, particularly as water for respiration passes
in through the mouth, over the gills and out
through the gill slits. If the fish is flat on its
belly, the mouth is pressed on the sea-bed and
the breathing current would pick up sand and
mud. In the skates we saw an adaptation in
which the water comes in through a special
spiracle on the top of the head and not through
the mouth. In the flatfish the problem has
been avoided by lying not on their bellies, but on
their sides. However, this produced another
problem: one eye would be pressed on to the
sea-bed so its vision would be very restricted.
The flatfishes avoid this problem in a unique
way: the lower eye moves over the top of the head
as the little fish grows so that it comes to lie
beside the other on the upper side. All flatfish
start life in the middle and surface layers of the
sea, and the migration of the eye takes place when
the fish changes its mode of life and becomes a
bottom-living creature. Some of the flatfish

lie on their left sides with both eyes on the right side, and in others the eye has moved to the left side and they lie on the right side. Associated with the bottom-living habit, the underside is white and the upper side carries a protective camouflage coloration.

The flatfish, like the members of the cod family, are of very great economic importance. At least five different species are commonly found on the fishmonger's slab. In consequence a great deal of work has been done on their natural history by fishery scientists.

The Turbot Family BOTHIDAE

The members of this family all lie on their right sides and the two eyes are on the left side. Three species are of economic importance and there are also a few deep-water species that are very seldom seen. The most sought-after commercial species is the **turbot**, *Scophthalmus maximus* (Plate 46). It has an excellent flavour and always commands a high price. In 1972 1050 tons worth £633,000 were landed in Britain. The turbot can be identified by means of three characteristics: it is a flatfish lying on its left side, its dorsal and anal fins do not continue underneath the tail, and it has tubercles but no scales on the upper eyed side. It is a large diamond-shaped fish of up to over 80 cm (32 in.) in length. The British rod-caught record is 14·174 kg (31¼ lb) for one caught in 1972 at the

Eddystone Lighthouse. The eyed side is light brown with many spots and speckles so that the fish matches well with its surroundings, which are usually sandy or gravelly bottoms of moderate depth. It is found all round Britain but is predominantly a resident of the shallow southern North Sea.

The food of the young turbot, before they change to the adult form and a life on the bottom, consists of planktonic crustacea, but once they have settled on the sea-bed they eat fish such as young haddock, whiting, pouting, sandeels, sprats, pilchards and dragonets.

Turbot spawn in the summer. The female is very prolific and, depending on size, she will produce up to ten million eggs. The planktonic eggs float in the upper water layers and hatch in a week to ten days. The young are symmetrical with an eye on each side. They continue to live in the plankton until they are about five months old, when the right eye moves to the left side and the young turbot takes to the bottom.

The **brill**, *Scophthalmus rhombus* (Plate 56), is the only fish likely to be confused with the turbot, and it can be distinguished because the upper eyed side is covered with scales and it does not have any tubercles. The British rod-caught record brill is 7·257 kg (16 lb) for one caught off the Isle of Man in 1950.

The brill is rounder than the turbot. The eyed upper side is brown, grey or greenish with darker variegations, and lighter spots and speckles. The underside, like that of the turbot, is an opaque white.

The brill is rare in Scottish waters but is common on sand and gravel in the inshore waters of southern England. The catches landed in Britain amounted to 200 tons in 1972 and were worth £68,000.

The food and breeding habits are very similar to those of the turbot.

The three species of topknot are very like young turbot and brill, but they can be distinguished easily because the dorsal and anal fins continue under the tail where they form two small lobes.

The **topknot**, *Zeugopterus punctatus* (Plate 51), is the commonest and largest of the three species. It grows to 25 cm (10 in.). The British rod-caught record is for one caught off Jersey, in 1972, which was 311 g (11 oz 2 dm). The body is almost a perfect oval. The dorsal and anal fins go nearly all round the fish. The scales on the eyed side are very rough. The colour is a rich brown with variegated blotches and marbling. There are two stripes by the eye and a dark spot behind the curve of the lateral line.

The topknot is found on rocky shores in shallow water. It often occurs among the seaweed *Laminaria* near low tide mark and on rough ground to 40 m (22 fathoms).

Bloch's topknot, *Phrynorhombus regius* (Plate 46), has the first ray of the dorsal fin longer than any of the others, and there is a single large spot on the lateral line near the tail. The rest of the eyed side is brown with irregular darker blotches. Bloch's topknot is the rarest of the three species and is found from low tide mark to 50 m (27 fathoms), mainly on the west coast. It grows to 20 cm (8 in.).

The **Norwegian topknot**, *Phrynorhombus norvegicus*, is found patchily all round Britain. It is common on rough ground but does not grow to more than 12 cm (5 in.), so is rarely caught. The upper surface is rough and sandy brown, with darker irregular markings.

The **megrim**, *Lepidorhombus whiffiagonis* (Plate 50), is a deep-water flatfish that is found mainly off the north, west and south-west coasts of Britain from 50 to 400 m (25–220 fathoms). It is sometimes seen in fish shops, after it has been landed by offshore trawlers.

The body of the megrim is narrow and thin. The eyes and the mouth are large, and the left eye—the one near the mouth—is slightly nearer the snout than the other. The upper side is yellowish brown with indistinct spots. It grows to 60 cm (24 in.) and the British rod-caught record of 1·644 kg (3 lb 10 oz) is held by one caught at Ullapool in 1966.

The food of young megrims consists mainly of bottom-living crustacea, and older ones chiefly eat fish, particularly Norway pout and sandeels.

The megrim has some commercial importance and 1050 tons, worth £123,000, were landed in

Britain in 1972. However, it is much inferior to turbot, sole and plaice in flavour.

Lepidorhombus boscii is another deep-water flatfish and it is so like the megrim that it has often been confused with that species. However, it has a pair of round spots on the dorsal and anal fins near the tail which the megrim does not possess. It grows to about 40 cm (16 in.).

The **scaldfish**, *Arnoglossus laterna* (Plate 46), gets its name from the ease with which its scales get lost when it is caught in a trawl. The scales are large and fragile, and when they have gone the fish appears as if it had been scalded. The scaldfish is oval with a smallish head and with smaller eyes and mouth than the megrim. It does not grow above 20 cm (8 in.). The upper side is grey or brown with irregular markings. It is common in the south of England, but is rare north of the Irish Sea and in the northern North Sea. It is found on sandy ground to about 120 m (66 fathoms). The scaldfish is too small to be of any economic value.

Two deep-water relatives of the scaldfish are *A. thori* and *A. imperialis*. Both are recorded from the south and west of the British Isles and can be recognized by the increased length of the first few rays of the dorsal fin in front of the right eye. All specimens should be referred to an expert for identification.

The Plaice Family   PLEURONECTIDAE

This family contains most of the commonly eaten

species of flatfish. All the species lie on their
left sides and the left eye moves over to the upper
right side. In one species (the flounder) there
are occasional specimens which lie on the right
side.

There are two groups of flatfish in this family.
In the first group the mouth is relatively small
and rarely extends beyond the beginning of the
eye. The most valuable member of this group
is the **plaice**, *Pleuronectes platessa* (Plate 56),
which is probably the best-known species of
flatfish. It can be identified easily because the
upper, eyed, side is smooth without any scales
on the lateral line or on the dorsal and anal fin
margins. Also it has a row of horny knobs
which lie between the eyes and the start of the
lateral line. Although these knobs are diagnostic,
the plaice is more usually distinguished by its
colour. The upper side is an olive greenish
brown with bright red or orange spots which
usually have a white or blue halo. There are
also a few dark brown spots and some cream ones.
The underside is a dull cream-white. The
lateral line has a very slight curve above the
pectoral fin. Plaice grow to 60 cm (24 in.) in
length, but most areas are so heavily fished that
few plaice have a chance to reach this size. The
British rod-caught record is held by a plaice
3·6 kg (7 lb 15 oz) caught at Salcombe in 1964.

Plaice are found abundantly all round the
British Isles. Very young fish of up to 6 cm
(2½ in.) are found close inshore in sandy bays,

but the adult plaice are found mainly on sand, and less often on gravel or mud, at depths down to 100 m (55 fathoms). Because of the great economic importance of plaice, much scientific work has been done by fishery biologists to learn about its natural history and what effects fishing has on the fish population and the recruitment of young plaice to the fishery.

Plaice spawn from December to April. One of the largest spawning areas is in the southern North Sea. Other smaller areas are located in Rye Bay and elsewhere in the Channel, off Flamborough Head, in the Firth of Forth, the Moray Firth and elsewhere in the northern North Sea, in the Bristol Channel, in Cardigan Bay and other grounds in the Irish Sea. There are many smaller spawning grounds round the coasts of Scotland and Ireland. The fertilized eggs, about 2 mm in diameter, float near the surface and hatch after fifteen to twenty-one days. The larvae, which are only 6·5 mm ($\frac{1}{4}$ in.) long, subsist for some time on the food stored in the yolk. This yolk, as in all other fish, provides the nourishment for the growing embryo in the egg and for the larval fish after hatching. In eight or nine days the yolk supply is nearly used up and the larva begins to feed, first on the microscopic plants called diatoms, and then on larger planktonic plants and animals. After about four weeks the little plaice has grown to 10 to 14 mm (about $\frac{1}{2}$ in.) and it begins to metamorphose, that is, change its shape. Until this time the larva has been a symmetrical fish with an eye on each side, but now the left eye begins to move to the top of the head and the whole snout takes on a twist. The eye moves over the top of the head on to the right side, and the little plaice goes down to the bottom to start its life as a flatfish. By this stage all the larvae have drifted from the spawning grounds to inshore nursery grounds. Those which spawned in the southern North Sea drift to the sandy shores of the Dutch and German coasts. After one summer inshore the plaice move out to deeper water.

The food of adult plaice consists mainly of bivalve molluscs such as cockles, mussels, clams, scallops and razor clams. Other animals such as small crabs, hermit crabs, shrimps, worms, brittle stars, and sea urchins are also eaten.

Plaice are mainly caught commercially in trawls and seine nets. In 1972 the British catch amounted to 41,800 tons, worth £7,997,000. Besides its importance to inshore and deep-sea fishermen, the plaice is a great favourite with the sea angler.

A flatfish that is often confused with the plaice is the **dab**, *Limanda limanda* (Plate 58). One source of confusion is that small plaice and flounders are collectively called dabs. However, the true dab can be distinguished easily by rubbing a finger from tail to head. The scales on the upper eyed side have backward-pointing teeth, so that the fish feels very rough. The identification should be confirmed by looking at the lateral line, which has a semi-circular curve by the pectoral fin. In the plaice and flounder the lateral line has only a slight bend by the pectoral fin.

The colour of the upper side of the dab is usually a light brown with darker spots and sometimes a few yellow or orange ones. The effect as a whole is to make the dab very inconspicuous when in its natural habitat of sandy bays and offshore banks. It is abundant all round Britain.

The dab is smaller than the plaice or flounder and very rarely exceeds 30 cm (12 in.).

The breeding of the dab is very similar to that of the plaice described above. Spawning is a little later, and the eggs, at 0·8 mm in diameter, are considerably smaller, but the stages of larval metamorphosis are very similar indeed.

The food of the dab is more varied than that of the plaice and includes more worms such as lugworms and bristle-worms, more crustacea such as shrimps, shore crabs and amphipods, and proportionately fewer bivalve molluscs.

The dab is caught in the nets of commercial inshore fishermen, and in 1972 they landed 1650 tons of dabs worth £169,000 in Britain. The dab is often caught by sea anglers and the British rod-caught record is for a dab caught at the Skerries in 1968 of 1·211 kg (2 lb 10¾ oz).

The **flounder**, *Platichthys flesus* (Plate 63), is another flatfish which is often confused with the plaice. Like the plaice, and unlike the dab, it has a smooth upper-eyed side, but it has three rows of sharp backward-pointing spines, which are diagnostic. One row of these spines is along the lateral line down the centre of the coloured side. The other two rows are at the base of the dorsal and anal fins. The body colour of the flounder is usually brownish olive-green on the upper-eyed side with a few pale orange spots. The lower side is a more opaque white than the slightly translucent white of the plaice. Although the majority of flounders lie on the left side, specimens on their right side are commoner than in other species of pleuronectids.

As well as being found in fully marine habitats, the flounder is a freshwater and estuarine fish. It is found all round the British Isles and is locally very abundant. Spawning always takes place in the sea and the young, after metamorphosis, move into estuaries, and then often into fresh water. They will swim up rivers and dykes for a considerable distance and remain in fresh water during adolescence. The adult fish enter fresh water less readily but are often found where the salinity is reduced. In early spring they migrate offshore to the spawning grounds.

The flounder grows to 50 cm (20 in.). It has a poor flavour compared with the plaice and is not landed in any quantity in Britain. In 1972 200 tons of flounders, worth £12,000, were landed. It is, however, popular with sea anglers and the British rod-caught record stands at 2·593 kg (5 lb 11½ oz) for one caught at Fowey in 1956.

The **lemon sole**, *Microstomus kitt* (Plate 59),

is much more oval in outline than the previous species. Its scales are smooth and the skin is very slimy. The head and mouth are both small. The curve of the lateral line round the pectoral fin is reminiscent of the dab, but the smoothness of the skin distinguishes the two species. The lemon sole has beautiful variegated and marbled patterns of green, orange and yellow on a brown background.

The lemon sole grows to 60 cm (24 in.) and has an excellent flavour. Although it is found all round Britain, it is most plentiful off northern and western coasts, and the Scottish catches contributed largely to the British landings of 3900 tons in 1972, worth £1,255,000. The lemon sole is occasionally caught by anglers and the British rod-caught record specimen of 990 g (2 lb 2 oz 15 dm) was caught off Douglas, Isle of Man, in 1971.

The food of the lemon sole is largely composed of polychaete worms, but small crustacea and molluscs are also eaten.

The spawning season is the latest of all the flatfishes and regularly lasts into July, or even later in the north. The eggs are less buoyant than in other species, but otherwise the development and metamorphosis at 1·5–2 cm (about ¾ in.) are generally similar to those of other flatfishes.

The **witch**, *Glyptocephalus cynoglossus* (Plate 62), is a deep-water flatfish found off northern and western Britain on muddy bottoms. It can be recognized by its oval body, small head, straight lateral line and uniform brown and smooth upper-eyed side. The underside is a rather dirty white.

The witch grows to about 40 cm (16 in.), which is reached in eight to ten years. It is not an important commercial species and the 1972 British catch amounted to 1050 tons, worth £126,000. It is sometimes caught by anglers, and the British rod-caught record is at 533 g (1 lb 2 oz 13 dm) for one caught at Colwyn Bay in 1967.

The next two species form the second group in the Pleuronectid family, and they are characterized by a very large mouth which extends back at least as far as the middle of the eye.

The smallest of these flatfish is the **long rough dab**, *Hippoglossoides platessoides* (Plate 55), which does not grow to more than 32 cm (12½ in.) and 250 g (9 oz), although off North America they grow to 60 cm (24 in.) and are an important commercial fish. The long rough dab has a large mouth and a uniform warm brown upper surface and rough scales. It is only found round the northern half of the British Isles where it is often abundant.

The breeding season in the Clyde area is during March and April. The eggs are very large but most of the space is occupied by a watery fluid, and the actual size of the egg is much smaller. After ten days to two weeks the larvae hatch and are about 5 mm long. Metamorphosis is complete when the young fish are about 2·5 cm (1 in.). About 50% of the females mature at three years old when they have reached 20 cm (8 in.) in length.

The next species in this group is the largest of the flatfishes, the **halibut**, *Hippoglossus hippoglossus* (Plate 54). It grows to over 250 cm (100 in.) and 180 kg (about 400 lb). It can be recognized, even when small, by its olive-green upper surface and the marked curve of the lateral line round the pectoral fin. The blind side is white.

The halibut is a deep-water fish which is found mainly in the Faroes, Iceland and Greenland areas, but it also occurs less commonly as far south as south-west Ireland and the northern North Sea. It frequents sandy or gravelly bottoms from 90 m (50 fathoms) to beyond the edge of the continental shelf. Halibut are said to spawn at 700 to 900 m (400–500 fathoms).

Although the halibut is a flatfish, when adult it feeds almost exclusively on fish and many of these are caught in mid-water.

The halibut is a very valuable commercial species. It is caught on long lines set on deep-water offshore banks. The British landings in 1972 amounted to 1850 tons, valued at £652,000. It is not often caught by anglers, but there is a British rod-caught record for one of 88·904 kg (196 lb) caught off Caithness in 1974.

The **Greenland halibut**, *Reinhardtius hippoglossoides*, is a more northern species recognizable by its straight lateral line and pigmented blind side.

The Soles SOLEIDAE

Whereas the species in the plaice family have mainly a northern distribution, which includes Britain and extends to the Bay of Biscay, the soles are a southern group of flatfish some of whose species are regularly found in Britain, and others are stragglers.

Soles differ from the other flatfish which lie on their left side, by having tongue-shaped bodies. The dorsal fin extends to the front of the rounded head. The mouth is towards the side of the head and has a curiously shaped downward curve.

Soles are difficult fish to identify, and the correct naming depends on very careful examination of a lot of rather obscure characteristics. The **sole**, *Solea solea* (Plate 57), is the commonest British species and can be identified by having all the following features: both pectoral fins are well developed and the one on the blind side is almost as large as the one on the eyed side; the dorsal and anal fins are joined to the tail fin by a membrane; the nostril on the blind side is small and inconspicuous; and there is a black spot without a white halo on the pectoral fin which reaches the fin margin. The colour of the sole is dark brown with variegated markings. It grows to 60 cm (24 in.).

The sole is found plentifully in the Channel and the North Sea as far north as the Moray Firth. On the west coasts it is found all round Ireland and in the Irish Sea, but it gets progressively scarcer further north. Soles are found most commonly on fine, sandy ground but also on sandy mud and gravel. In the summer they are found in sandy bays and even in estuaries, but in winter they go to deeper pits in otherwise shallow areas.

The sole is believed to feed almost entirely by night and to lie half buried in the sand during the day. It is said that at night soles find their food by smell and touch, by means of the numerous feelers on the underside of the head. The food consists mainly of worms, particularly those kinds which dwell in sandy tubes on the bottom, but brittle stars and other echinoderms are also eaten, as well as some bivalve molluscs and crustacea.

Soles spawn from February to the early summer. The eggs are said to hatch in ten days and the yolk is divided into different segments. The young larvae have an air-bladder but, as in all flatfish, it is absent in the adult. Metamorphosis takes place at 13 mm ($\frac{1}{2}$ in.).

The sole is a very valuable fish and is generally accepted as the best-flavoured sea fish. Although not landed in large quantities, it is very much sought after. The catches in 1972 amounted to 1350 tons, worth £1,101,000. It is not an important anglers' fish but is sometimes caught.

The British rod-caught record is 1·913 kg (4 lb 3½ oz) for one caught off Redcliffe Beach in 1974.

The **sand sole**, *Pegusa lascaris* (Plate 57), is very similar to the ordinary sole and shares with it the following two features: the pectoral fin on the blind side is well developed and only slightly smaller than that on the eyed side, and the dorsal and anal fins are joined to the tail by a membrane. However, the nostril on the blind side of the sand sole is very much larger than the nostril on the eyed side and is in the form of a 'rosette'; the black spot on the upper pectoral fin is surrounded by a halo and does not reach the fin margin. These two characteristics distinguish the sand sole from *S. solea*. The colour of the upper side is a light reddish brown with numerous orange and black flecks.

The sand sole rarely grows to more than 40 cm (16 in.). It is found on inshore sandy grounds. It is a rare fish which is occasionally caught in the Channel and very seldom elsewhere.

In the next two species the pectoral fins on the blind side are minute and may indeed be difficult to see. The species can be distinguished by the size of the eyes. In the **solenette**, *Buglossidium luteum* (Plate 60), the eyes are very small. It is also a small fish which, even when adult, does not often exceed 12 cm (5 in.). It can be distinguished from the young of *S. solea* because the dorsal and anal fins are not joined to the caudal fin by a membrane. The colour of the eyed side is light sandy brown with a few speckles. Every fifth or sixth ray on the dorsal and anal fins are black.

The solenette is found all round the British Isles on sandy inshore ground, but is not common in the north, though in the southern North Sea, the Channel and Irish Sea it is extremely common.

The **thick-back sole**, *Microchirus variegatus* (Plate 60), also has a minute pectoral fin on the blind side and no membranes joining the caudal to the anal and dorsal fins, but it has large eyes. It grows to 23 cm (9 in.). The eyed side is a warm brown with about five transverse bars running across the body. The size of the eyes and the colouring are sufficient to distinguish this species from the solenette.

The thick-back sole is not found in the North Sea and is not common in the north or west of Scotland. It is only caught regularly off Devon and Cornwall, where it is found on sandy ground offshore.

The Triggerfish   BALISTIDAE

The **triggerfish**, *Balistes carolinensis*, is a very rare fish with a deep laterally compressed body and two dorsal fins, the first of which has a very rough-edged first spine. The mouth is very small with large protruding teeth. The triggerfish migrates northwards in summer and is caught off south-west England and Ireland. One was

caught in Swanage Bay, Dorset, in 1973, and at
1·871 kg (4 lb 2 oz) holds the British rod-caught
record.

The Puffer-fish TETRAODONTIDAE

The **puffer-fish**, *Lagocephalus lagocephalus*, can
be identified immediately by the spines which
thickly cover the whole underside from the throat
to the tail. The back is dull blue and the belly
white. It is a rare oceanic fish which occasionally turns up on the Channel coast, and the south
and south-western coasts of Ireland.

The Sunfishes MOLIDAE

There are two species in this family which occur
in British waters. Both are very oddly shaped.
The **sunfish**, *Mola mola* (Plate 61), is reported
fairly regularly, though nearly all the records are
of dying specimens feebly attempting to swim
on their sides. It is commonest off the west
coasts and is said to have been so abundant at one
time that the Aran Islanders hunted it with
harpoons, but this was probably quite exceptional.
Certainly, round the rest of Britain and in the
North Sea, it is a rare straggler, probably from
warmer oceanic waters to the south.

The sunfish when seen sideways on is almost
circular, because although it has a caudal fin, it

appears to have no tail. The single dorsal and anal fins are tall and narrow. The adult sunfish is huge. It sometimes reaches 150 cm (5 ft) in length and 226 kg (500 lb) in weight, but specimens of 274 cm (9 ft) and even 330 cm (11 ft) have been recorded. It is a greyish brown above and paler below.

The **truncated sunfish**, *Ranzania laevis*, is an even rarer species that has been reported from Cornwall and south-west Ireland. It, too, is an oceanic wanderer that arrives in Britain through some misfortune. It is smaller than the sunfish and rarely exceeds 80 cm (30 in.). The body is longer but nevertheless has the bizarre cut-off tail.

The Clingfish GOBIESOCIDAE

In these little shore fishes there is a sucker on the underside formed from the pelvic fins. An account of the different forms of suckers in the different families has been given on page 121. The sucker of the clingfishes is large and very powerful, and with it the fish attaches itself firmly to rocks and stones.

Like so many other shore fishes, the clingfish lay their eggs in empty bivalve shells or in rock crevices. The elongate eggs are usually laid in clusters and then guarded by the male until they hatch. The larvae drift in the plankton.

The clingfish can be identified as a small fish

of less than 7·5 cm (3 in.) with a sucker and elongate shape. There are, however, four species which are not easy to identify. They fall into two groups.

In the first group the dorsal and anal fins do not run near the caudal fin but are quite separate. In the **small-headed clingfish**, *Apletodon microcephalus*, the dorsal fin commences directly above the anal. It has a patchy distribution in Cornwall and western Scotland. In the second species in this group, the **two-spotted clingfish**, *Diplecogaster bimaculata* (Plate 43), the dorsal fin commences just in front of the start of the anal fin. It is found all round Ireland, on the western coasts of England and Wales and on the western and northern Scottish coasts. It is a highly coloured orange-red, with blue, violet, brown and yellow markings, but the coloration is very variable.

In the second group of clingfishes the dorsal and anal fins are not well separated from the caudal fin. In the **shore clingfish**, *Lepadogaster lepadogaster* (Plate 43), the fins actually join. It is a red or purplish fish spotted with brown, but the colours of the clingfishes are so variable that they cannot be relied on for identification. The shore clingfish is found on rocky coasts among boulders and seaweeds, and is common on the western coasts of Britain between tide marks. Breeding takes place during the early summer when the golden eggs are laid in clumps on the undersides of stones. They are guarded by either parent. The larvae are planktonic during July and August.

In the **Connemara clingfish**, *Lepadogaster candollei* (Plate 43), the dorsal and anal fins end close to, but are not joined to, the caudal fin. The body is red with contrasting yellow fins and bright red spots on the top of the head. It is a rather rare fish which is found on rocky shores below low water mark among seaweed. It is reported from Cornwall, South Wales, southern and western Ireland and parts of western Scotland.

The Angler Fish LOPHIIDAE

The **angler fish**, *Lophius piscatorius* (Plate 64), is one of the most remarkable bottom-living fishes. It has a grotesque shape with a huge mouth, many teeth and a flabby jelly-like body. The mouth has an enormous gape. The first fin ray of the dorsal fin is situated on the snout and forms a fishing rod complete with a lure, composed of a flap of skin, on the end of the line. The way in which an angler fish waves the lure and attracts its prey within range of the enormous mouth has been described from fish kept in the Plymouth aquarium, so there can be no doubt about the use to which it is put. The angler fish is a voracious feeder and mainly consumes fish. The list of its recorded prey is a very long one which includes dogfish, skate, cod, haddock, whiting, herring, sprats, sandeels, flatfish and many others.

Beside the large head, the body appears rather puny, and is covered with a loose, smooth skin. Each small pectoral fin is rather like a limb. The gill openings are small and below the pectoral fins. The body is brownish grey with many speckles and variegated markings, so that in its natural habitat on the sea-bed, the angler is incredibly well camouflaged. It is found mainly on gravelly bottoms all round the British Isles.

The angler breeds in the spring and lays a huge mucilaginous raft in which up to a million eggs may be embedded. These gelatinous sheets may be up to 9 m (30 ft) long and 90 cm (3 ft) wide. The baby anglers are planktonic.

The angler is usually about 45 cm (18 in.) in length, but specimens of 198 cm (78 in.) have been recorded. The British rod-caught record is for an angler of 33.791 kg (74 lb 8 oz) caught in 1972 S.W. of the Eddystone Lighthouse.

The angler fish is edible and it is landed regularly by British fishing boats. In 1972 3800 tons were landed.

INDEX

Made and printed by William Clowes & Sons, Limited
London, Beccles and Colchester